AF362487

WORLD BALANCE SHEET

GLOBAL ASSETS AT A GLANCE

HARALD DEUTSCH

WorldBalanceSheet.org

WorldBalanceSheet.org
Harald Deutsch
Am Wasserbett 12
68526 Ladenburg
Germany
Telephone: +49 172 3030 837
Website: www.worldbalancesheet.org
Email: info@worldbalancesheet.org

ISBN: 978-3-9821906-0-0
eISBN: 978-3-9821906-1-7
1st edition 2020
The German National Library catalogs this publication in the German National Bibliography. Detailed bibliographic information can be found on http://dnb.ddb.de.

About the Author

Harald Deutsch, M.D., M.Sc., is an award-winning strategy consultant, who has advised governments and corporations in many countries for more than 20 years. He currently works as a strategic advisor, non-executive director, and investor. He has worked as a partner, managing director, vice president, and global practice leader for some of the world's leading consultancy firms.

In 2019, he founded WorldBalanceSheet.org, where he currently serves as president.

WorldBalanceSheet.org is a non-profit think tank that focuses on scientific works on general global economic issues that are insufficiently covered by other sources. Real economy matters are particularly studied, which are independent of political–economic systems. WorldBalanceSheet.org is uncompromisingly focused on pure professional and academic standards; it is independent and unpolitical. Its members are comprised of economists and academics of various disciplines. This book is the first publication supported by WorldBalanceSheet.org.

Acknowledgments

I would like to thank the members of WorldBalanceSheet.org who played central roles in ensuring the quality and impartiality of this work. Their support was crucial for the success.

I would like to thank Clemens Deutsch for his dedication in providing his analysis of the world's pension systems that formed the cornerstone of Chapter 8.2 Pensions. Furthermore, he has spent many hours discussing intricate analytical and numerical issues with me. Peter Heupel gave important insights into Chapter 5 Property, specifically for subsoil assets and urban land. Laurenz Rath contributed his expertise in fixed assets to improve Chapter 6 Plant, Equipment, Inventories. Furthermore, Vincent Druffel-Spinola supported general quality improvements. I thank the whole team for their contributions, discussions, and recommendations.

Furthermore, I would like to thank some deep thinkers who influenced and motivated me for this work. Professor in Economics of Innovation and Public Value at University College London, Mariana Mazzucato focused her unrivaled work on central issues about the value, challenging the scientific community. WorldBalanceSheet.org was founded to deal with some of these challenges. Professor in Money and Macroeconomics at the University of Frankfurt, Michael P. Evers was patient in our discussions. He helped me to understand important economic concepts in this work and their limits. Deputy Director General International and European Relations of the European Central Bank, Livio Stracca helped me integrate monetary theory and central bank policies.

Finally, I would like to thank my family for their patience and support. My son, Lars, leveraged his technical experience to improve our web presence. Most importantly, my biggest thanks go to my wife, Yvonne, for her unwavering support and encouragement, not to mention the regular supply of delicious food. I could not have done this work without you.

Abbreviations

BIS	Bank for International Settlement
CAGR	Compound annual growth rate
CFA	Commodity flow analysis
DB	Defined benefit plan
DC	Defined contribution plan
EC	European Commission
FAO	Food and Agriculture Organization of the United Nations
FED	Federal Reserve System
FTE	Full-time equivalent
GDP	Gross domestic product
GIFT	Global Intangible Finance Tracker
GNI	Gross national income
ICT	Information, communication, and telecommunications
IP	Intellectual property
IT	Information technology
IFPRI	International Food Policy Research Institute
IFRS	International Financial Reporting Standards
IMF	International Monetary Fund
IMPACT	International Model for Policy Analysis of Agricultural Commodities and Trade
NGO	Non-governmental organization
NPV	Net present value
NWFP	Non-wood forest products
OECD	Organisation for Economic Co-operation and Development

P+L	Profit and loss statement
PIM	Perpetual inventory method
PMI	Post-merger integration
PPP	Purchasing Power Parity
PWT	Penn World Table
SALM	Sovereign asset and liability management
SEEA	System of Environmental-Economic Accounting
SEEA-CF	System of Environmental-Economic Accounting–Central Framework
SIPRI	Stockholm International Peace Research Institute
SME	Small and medium-sized enterprise
SNA	System of National Accounts
SOE	State-owned enterprise
SPDR	Standard and Poor's Depositary Receipt
tn	trillion
UN	United Nations
UNCTAD	United Nations Conference on Trade and Development
US GAAP	Generally Accepted Accounting Principles in the US

Contents

Executive Summary

Why do we need a World Balance Sheet?

The composition and distribution of global wealth are among the most frequently discussed topics today. But what do we really know about the world's capital? To the best of our knowledge, this book is the first to produce a financial balance sheet of the world. We address the following core questions at the heart of the global economy. What is the value of global capital? How is it composed? Does it sustainably support humankind's standard of living?

Why is this work new? Traditionally, the world economy is not measured. National economies are measured; global values are created as summations of all country values. And the economic strength is primarily measured by production. Gross domestic product (GDP) is the key metric; balance sheets are not a typical tool for managing economies. This history has led to the surprising finding that, in 2020, an integrated balance sheet of the world has not been established in the universe of economic data surrounding us.

Thus, why is a World Balance Sheet important? Firstly, in a real economy, global assets are the world's production factors that generate all economic outputs. What is the importance of these production factors and their relative contribution? Do we see changes, potentially declines? What does it take to promote them? Do we see structural changes that we need to address with structural answers?

Secondly, from a political-economic perspective, the world's assets encompass everything around us - our house and the streets surrounding it, our car, the company we are working for, our children's school, and the work of our hands. Are all of these in good order? Are there issues to be politically addressed?

We cannot manage what we do not measure. Therefore, we need to measure the world's capital.

World Balance Sheet: Numerical outcome

In chapters 3–10, we develop a structure and construct numbers for the World Balance Sheet, as shown in Fig. 1. As of December 31, 2018, the world's total capital is 1,497.46 trillion USD (2014), of which 45.9% (687.52 tn USD) are commercial assets and 54.1% (809.94 tn USD) are human capital. This total capital supports the world's current consumption with future annual growth of 1.13%. We are cautiously confident that despite certain inaccuracies, the total results are reliable within a confidence interval. No major capital gaps remain since consumption and total assets are balanced.

The key learnings of our study are the following:

- Land value is strongly concentrated. That is, urban land represents 65% of the land's value but less than 1% of the area. Furthermore, 32.2% of the value is attributed to agricultural land. The huge price differences drive conversion into urban land (urban sprawl) and transformation of forests and protected areas into agricultural land. This value concentration has increased in the past years.

World Balance Sheet December 31, 2018 (in tn USD)	
Assets	**1,497.46**
Fixed assets	**638.99**
Property	**184.01**
Land	132.09
Cropland	26.45
Pasture land	16.06
Forest	2.69
Barren land	1.00
Urban land	85.89
Subsoil assets	51.91
Oil	30.79
Gas	3.73
Coal	6.85
Minerals (10)	10.54
Plant	**260.27**
Dwellings	119.84
Other buildings	140.43
Equipment	**50.73**
Commercial equipment	41.98
Military equipment	8.74
Intangible assets	**143.99**
Goodwill	117.63
Listed companies, disclosed	8.00
Listed companies, acquired	35.92
SMEs, acquired	72.73
SOEs, acquired	0.99
Intellectual property	20.76
Brand value, licenses	5.60
(Global governance)	(4.88)
Current assets	**48.54**
Inventories	**46.90**
Commercial inventories	17.54
Consumer durables	29.36
Cash and cash equivalents	**1.64**
Monetary gold reserves	1.41
Gold SPDR holdings	0.10
Crypto currencies	0.13
Human capital	**809.94**
Liabilities and Equity	**1,497.46**
Consumption (@1,13% CAGR)	1,497.46

Figure 1: World Balance Sheet

- Subsoil assets are still relatively low-value; only oil represents a major value. Mining is more attractive than recycling given the low relative value of minerals. The growth of this asset class is similar to that of the world economic growth (except coal, which slightly declines).
- Tangible assets, such as buildings, equipment, and inventories, represent approximately half of the commercial assets. However, they are highly concentrated in cities in advanced economies.
- Intangible assets amount to 143.99 tn USD. This significant position stems from the evaluation of the world's intangible assets in more than 200 million companies.
- Human capital forms the largest part of the world's total capital. However, its relative share is diminishing. The share of commercial capital grows, which is driven by volume increases as well as by price increases (asset inflation).
- The world's total assets support the consumption level of humankind with a growth rate of 1.13%. This rate is less than the average growth of the past years (2.74%) due to two factors. Firstly, natural resources (e.g., forest and seas) are overexploited, resulting in declining values. Secondly, the gradual growth in human capital is mainly due to the ageing population in industrial countries. Both have a diminishing effect on consumption growth.

Key points in economic theory and statistics

Methodologically, we develop the World Balance Sheet using two balance sheets. We first introduce the thought experiment of World Inc., where they acquire all global organizations, assets, and everything of commercial value. Then, they consolidate all these acquisitions in their balance sheet, in which International Financial Reporting Standards (IFRS) rules are applied.

However, World Inc.'s balance sheet cannot comprehensively account for the world's capital. We need to consider the balance sheet of World Inc.'s shareholders who comprise all private households constituting the humankind. This balance sheet is complementary to that of World Inc. with regard to asset classes and value drivers. The humankind owns its human capital, and the entire equity of World Inc. It needs, however, to fund its future consumption. Therefore, the rules of household balance sheets are applied. We apply one homogeneous methodology, outlined in chapters 3 and 4.

The core theoretical learnings are the following:

- The global economy is a closed economy. Only one globe exists, which has no external trade. Our primary global view allows the application of global accounting identities, which is not possible in national accounting. This leads to important structural insights.
- A list of natural assets emerges, which constitutes the World Balance Sheet's structure. This finding is important considering that previous studies about the world's capital used various scopes and methodologies, leading to different and arbitrary asset structures. However, the World Balance Sheet's asset list is not our arbitrary design. This asset list forms a natural subset of all IFRS asset classes.
- Large intangible assets are a challenge to economic theory. Although these assets are intangible in nature, they form a part of real economy. The market value of more than 200 million companies exceeds their book value by more than 100 tn USD, mainly accounted for as goodwill. However, what capital does this goodwill represent on a collective level? Statistical data quality and scientific activity are not in accordance with the significance of this asset class.
- Financial assets are not involved in the World Balance Sheet due to accounting identities. All economic activity happens and is funded in the present. Debt is irrelevant in the real economy. A burden for future generations is not created; this situation is only a popular illusion.
- Only a few money types remain in the World Balance Sheet, namely, gold and truly produced cyber currencies, such as Bitcoin, whose role is limited quantitatively. All national

currencies, as fiat currencies, vanish due to accounting identities.

There are also insights into data sources and their quality.

We utilized more than 100 sources, which are aligned with our selected approach. Data gaps and accuracy risks are discussed in detail in Chapter 4. Based on this assessment, we have set up a three-tier architecture of the sources used that is headed by the World Bank, United Nations (UN), and International Monetary Fund (IMF).

In general terms, we find accuracy risks higher than typically discussed in economic literature based on the following concepts:

- Many economic statistics are fraught with spurious accuracy. Contrary to science, economic data are not provided with error bars and confidence intervals as they focus more on precision than on accuracy.
- The system of national accounts (SNA) is Janus-faced. It is the dominant accounting framework of international economic statistics and therefore the most important data source for this study. However, we find it only partially usable for our work.
- Firstly, it focuses on production, not on assets, and assets are indirectly modeled, not directly measured. Furthermore, the applied modeling methods are partly obsolete and overly simple. The use of these methods, along with slow and incoherent reporting, leads to considerable accuracy risks.
- Secondly, SNA's concept of asset is not identical to that of IFRS. This difference is particularly significant for government- and consumer-owned assets and also for specific asset classes (e.g., intangible assets).
- With regard to public capital, the differences between SNA and IFRS's treatment on public assets cannot be easily bridged. A valid consistent theory frankly is not existing. In Chapter 4.4. possible levers for improvement are discussed.

- Major positions in the World Balance Sheet have limited data sources and are not appropriately covered by literature, for example, urban land, military equipment, intangible assets, and consumer durables.

Takeaways for political economy and beyond

Although we focus on the real economy and its accounting, not on the political economy, some interesting findings are relevant for political decision-makers.

Firstly, ecological challenges are emerging in the world's capital structure. In a commercially conservative manner, we have consciously refrained from accounting for ecological services (see Chapter 5). Still, the value of forests is falling. The seas' value is neglectable because fishing revenues are outweighed by ecological issues and the lack of global governance. An economically reasoned concept for defending the value of those assets is missing, yet. Here, the output-oriented SNA results in disadvantages for political decision-making.

Human capital seems to diminish compared with commercial capital. Total capital's quota of 54.1% has fallen in the last years and is expected to decline further due to several factors. Human capital is mainly contributed by high-income countries, where labor force ages and real wage growth tends to be flat. Recently, several authors reported that the share of labor income compared with capital income is falling which is supported by our results.

Inequality may progress more than publicly perceived. As the most evenly distributed asset, human capital is in relative decline, whereas commercial assets, particularly property and intangible assets, have a higher growth rate than the overall economy. A post-industrial knowledge economy arises: Software substitute tangible products. Intellectual property (IP) substitutes plants. Tangible assets are substituted by intangible assets. However, these asset types are most concentrated, that is, only a few own these assets. Therefore, the secular growth of these asset classes drives inequality. However, this concern cannot be handled by conventional social contracts any more. The tools of the industrial society do not suffice to manage the post-modern labor-capital relationship. These tools were developed during the 19th and 20th centuries, e.g., workers' councils and labor unions. Social engineering tools for the new rising asset classes are waiting for their development.

Intangible assets pose a theoretical challenge in this context. At present, they account for 9.6% of the total capital and 20.9% of commercial assets. However, intangible assets are poorly understood and patchily reported. What capital do intangible assets, particularly goodwill, reflect?

To address these questions, additional improved data are required. The earth's surface (511 million km^2) has been known with great accuracy for centuries. However, we cannot determine the world's total capital (i.e., 1,497.46 tn USD) earlier than now. We cannot expect the numerical results of this first World Balance Sheet to be completely accurate in every detail. Rather, the overall accuracy is probably not much better than a few percentage points that need to be refined.

Government balance sheets need to be created; physical inventories need to be conducted. Unmonitored sizeable assets require considerable attention, for example, urban land, non-listed companies, public assets, military equipment, and consumer durables.

Although expensive global science projects such as Human Genome and Human Brain are conducted, no such projects for human wealth have been created. This is not appropriate as we cannot manage what we do not measure. Therefore, a global data capturing project for human wealth should be set up.

2

Introduction

> "If we cannot define what we mean by value, we cannot be sure to produce it, nor to share it fairly, nor to sustain economic growth."
>
> (MARIANA MAZZUCATO 2018, XIX).

2.1 MEASURING THE VALUE OF THE GLOBAL ECONOMY

We live in a world shaped by global capitalism. The importance of the economy to the people is evidenced by the abundance of financial and economic data. The news reports daily about capital markets and financial transactions. People deal with thousands of financial figures everywhere, and every day. Every economic item seems to be measured, reported, and managed.

However, this is not true. A closer examination shows that economic data are amassed based on two principles.

The first principle is fragmentariness. The scope of each economic statistic is limited a priori because it contains information about a country, a company or a political institution. Only in favorable cases, global data are available. These data are then integrated ex-post from hundreds of country data. The economy does not have a primary global view.

At the end of the 15th century, globes were invented, which have allowed immediate intellectual access to a primary global view of the world. Although unknown areas can be seen on the globe as white spots, it was clear from the beginning that the Earth is round, what size the white spots were, and where they were located. Global perspective has been encouraged from scratch.

Economically, we still live in the cartographic world of the 14th century. Our world map of economic data is flat and glued together from regionally drawn partial maps. It is rarely clear, if you see the entire world or only a part of it. Do you need 41, 141, or all 194 countries to sum up a worldwide statistic? Where are the economic white spots? Are they sizeable? If you closely examine our economic world map, you can see all the junctures, slightly different scales, and styles of various economic cartographers.

And secondly, economic data are centered about value flows. Economic output is in the focus. That is, how much revenues and profit a company generates? What is the GDP of a country? What tax revenues does this GDP generate? Statistics and data about the foundations of the economic machine, their capital structure and assets, are limited.

However, a true global view of the world's capital structure is indispensable due to certain reasons.

Firstly, the real economic perspective exists. The world's assets are the production factors of global businesses. Judgment of every business requires two views, namely, the profit and loss statement (P+L) and the balance sheet. P+L gives evidence about the output, whereas the balance sheet shows the basis of this output. What are the production factors for the world's economy? What is their relative importance? How do they develop over time? What can we do to influence their development? Is it sufficient to address single developments, or do structural changes in the world economy require structural answers?

Secondly, in a political–economic perspective, global assets encompass everything of value surrounding us. Thus, are these values in good shape? The collapse of the Soviet Union and the communist economic system was initially noticeable in the erosion of infrastructure, the overexploitation of natural resources and the growing innovation gap. All of this means a huge decline in the capital base. This situation went unnoticed because this capital base was not adequately measured. Almost all observers from the west and east in 1989-1990 were not only surprised by the political developments, but also by the massive erosion of the economic structures, which led to an immediate and unexpected economic collapse. No valid capital figures had alerted these observers beforehand.

How is the situation today in our capitalistic world? Do we have well-maintained infrastructure, buildings, and equipment? Do our natural resources have high economic value? Therefore, what ecological measures are economically appropriate for the world community? What is the role of human capital? Does humankind have capable labor power, or does it need measures to nurture the resources through educational and healthcare efforts? Output centricity holds that melting the family's silver and selling it could be a sustainable source of income. Obviously, this is a misperception. Is there any recent rational evidence that we may melt some silver of the humankind? If so, we should take actions to measure it.

Ignorance of global capital structure entails not only risks but opportunity costs. What are the quantitative roles of new forms of economy derived from the Internet, software, and the knowledge society? What is the contribution of intangible assets? How can these better be exploited?

Therefore, we ask: What is the world's capital?

Surprisingly, no answer has yet been given. Instead, several partial responses were given from two perspectives.

Since Adam Smith wrote his famous *Wealth of Nations*, a governmental, a national view on the world's assets has been established.

(Finally, the title of the book was neither *Wealth of the World* nor *Wealth of the Humankind*.)

Which wealth do the nations control? Recently, scholars of the World Bank have given their answer in their latest report on The Changing Wealth of Nations 2018 (Lange, Wodon, and Carey 2018). According to the World Bank, nations control natural resources and fixed assets. In this perspective, the world's commercial capital amounts to 411 tn USD (2014). Shares or bonds are not within the scope of nations; these are managed by wealthy individuals.

Consequently, the perspective of wealthy individuals is represented in studies, such as the wealth reports published annually by Cap Gemini, Allianz, BCG, and other consultancies and financial institutions (Brandmeir et al. 2018; CapGemini 2018; Shorrocks 2018; Zakrzewski et al. 2018). Which wealth do the wealthy own? The wealthy possess shares, bonds, and real estate. Depending on the source and detailed scope, these accounts range from 160 tn USD to 210 tn USD (2018) globally. The wealthy do not own natural resources or human capital; these accounts are managed by the World Bank.

Global wealth perspectives differ in scope, methodology, and data sources. Asset categories and their definition vary among studies, already on their highest levels. That is, the fundamental question of what is capital and how it is composed has no agreement. Resulting figures diverge substantially, and cannot be easily compared.

This situation is not irresolvable. The value of the global economy can be measured using three methodological levers. Firstly, a helicopter view is applied as it covers all global assets, ideally without exception. Secondly, a simple, homogeneous, and standardized methodology beyond scientific disputation is required. Lastly, sufficient and reliable data sources are needed for quantitative computation.

Using the helicopter view, we observe the world and its various assets accounted by the World Bank and wealth reports as having no value. These assets are the white spots in the world's global wealth maps. What is the value of more than 30 million km² barren land? What is the value of unexplored subsoil assets? What is the value of the world's cultural heritage, such as the Acropolis and the Colosseum? What is the value of the world's military equipment, such as warships and tanks? What is the value of more than 1 bn used cars owned by private households? What is the value of more than 200 million private businesses beyond book value?

Thus far, the mainstream answer of global data aggregators in these and other instances has been zero. This finding is not satisfactory. Of course, the neglect of many assets is not compulsory.

The widely spread neglect is partly driven by the applied methodology. The dominant methodology in global accounting is the system of national accounts (SNA). However, this accounting model is only partially useful for any capital measurements. Assets belong to individuals, not to nations.

Therefore, commercial accounting dominates theory and practice of real existing capitalism, not national accounting. When the Italian mathematician Luca Pacioli described double-entry accounting in his best-selling book in 1494, it had been in use already for at least 200 years. Since then, commercial accounting has spread throughout the world and has proven beneficial and reliable for commercial activities, irrespective of the political–economic system. This method includes the evaluation of a multitude of assets. Therefore, we use commercial accounting as defined by the IFRS as the basis for evaluating the world's assets. We apply this methodology by acquiring all assets like a merchant would do.

Finally, sufficient data provision has been established only recently. Most studies used as data sources have been created in the last four years. Only five years ago, this work would have been impossible due to insufficient data.

2.2   OBJECTIVE OF THIS WORK

To **create** a financial balance sheet of the world economy **covering** all assets **using** a homogeneous, simple, and well-defined methodology.

2.3   STRUCTURE OF THIS BOOK

Chapter 3 introduces the thought experiment of World Inc., acquiring all global organizations, buying all global assets, and consolidating all economic values in its balance sheet. We find that in a fiat money system, this process can be financed by a central bank. Thus, the thought experiment can be conducted in principle. We set up the principles of the acquisition: We buy at market prices; and we do not alter the world economy as it is. Furthermore, we define the principles of the consolidation process, and we consolidate according to the IFRS framework, without loss of generality.

We find that IFRS categorizes two asset classes, namely, monovalent and bivalent assets. Monovalent assets are reported in only one balance sheet, for example, as inventories. They are acquired once by World Inc. and are reported in the final balance sheet at market prices. In contrast, bivalent assets are reported in two balance sheets (as asset and liability, respectively). They should theoretically offset due to accounting identities and are subject to the balance sheet consolidation process.

Chapter 4 gives an overview of the most important data sources and literature. It further briefly describes the SNA and its partial usefulness for this work. However, SNA has certain limitations by design, which include focus on production (not assets), built-in issues in the treatment of governmental and household assets, limited international homogeneity, and inconsistent and delayed reporting. Therefore, SNA data do not cover all asset classes, and data accuracy shows caveats. Furthermore, data sources are introduced and qualified. Weaknesses of data provision are highlighted. We find, that weaknesses of data availability are accompanied by weaknesses of theoretical foundations, for example, in the areas of unexplored natural resources, public assets, intangible assets, and consumer durables.

Chapter 5 examines monovalent assets, particularly land and subsoil assets. We will develop methodology and data, which rely partly on significant and detailed work of the World Bank. Some accounting issues are also highlighted. For instance, unexplored subsoil assets and land (e.g., sea grounds and polar regions) are not well-reflected in mainstream data sources. In general, the value of property can be evaluated comparably well, except for urban and barren land.

Chapter 6 is dedicated to the monovalent asset classes categorized as plant, equipment, and inventories. Data are collected from SNA and refined by the UN, World Bank, IMF, Organisation for Economic Co-operation and Development (OECD), and other organizations and authors. SNA names these asset classes as produced assets. This basis needs to be complemented with specific analyses of military equipment and consumer durables, which are underreported in SNA.

Chapter 7 discusses intangible assets and focuses on companies acquired by World Inc. These include listed companies, but as well all private businesses and state-owned enterprises (SOEs). Intangible assets, which are openly defined, include monovalent assets such as brand value, IP, and licenses. These assets are held in company balance sheets. However, intangible assets also include goodwill, which results from the consolidation of the bivalent asset class equity. The discrepancy between market value and book value of equity remains in World Inc.'s balance sheet as goodwill. Due to the large number of acquired companies, goodwill accounts to approximately one-sixth of World Inc.'s assets.

Chapter 8 discusses consolidation of bivalent assets. These accounts are acquired by World Inc. as assets and liabilities. The consolidation process does not always lead to offsetting (as one would expect from accounting identities). Instead, consolidation of debt, and consolidation of pensions lead to remaining balance sheet entries.

Chapter 9 treats the asset class cash and cash equivalent - money, in economic terminology. Also, the world's central banks, with their large balance sheets, are acquired by World Inc. However, this asset class has low value, because all national currencies of the world are fiat currencies. This phenomenon makes them bivalent assets that offset during the consolidation process. Only cyber currencies, such as Bitcoin, remain, which are monovalent (truly produced) assets. Furthermore, monetary gold is also accounted for as cash equivalent.

Chapter 10 - Synthesis - consolidates the results of the previous chapters as World Inc.'s balance sheet is complete. Shareholders' perspective is added by introducing the Balance Sheet of Humankind. The humankind finally possesses their human capital, pension claims, and all World Inc.'s equity. In theory, their assets should equal the net present value (NPV) of their consumption. Empirically, this can be confirmed. Based on previous work of the World Bank our computation shows that the world's total assets support the foreseeable consumption, even with a compound annual growth rate (CAGR) of 1.13%.

No asset gaps remain. Therefore, we are cautiously confident, that despite the different sources of inaccuracy the total results are reliable within a confidence interval.

Chapter 11 – Outlook - gives an overview of the theoretical implications of this work and provides an opportunity for future work in some areas. Although the difference between monovalent and bivalent assets is fundamental, value theory does not appropriately cover such difference. Also, the theoretical foundations of intangible assets, public capital, and quantitative easing need further investigation.

Furthermore, data reliability needs to be improved and data source errors diminished. Within the SNA, measurement of existing value needs more focus. Government balance sheets need to be created;

physical inventories need to be conducted; and accounting models with questionable accuracy (e.g., perpetual inventory method [PIM], commodity flow analysis [CFA]) should be eliminated.

Ideally, a global data capturing project for human wealth should be set up.

3

World Balance Sheet: The Model

3.1 WORLD INC.

World Inc. is a fictional public company that starts with an empty balance sheet. Thus, it has no assets and liabilities but has one logical share with a nominal zero value. Then, it acquires the entire world economy in a well-defined thought experiment. After this acquisition process, following the IFRS principles, all commercial capital of the world economy is reflected in World Inc.'s balance sheet.

3.2 ACQUISITION PROCESS

World Inc. acquires the world's entire economic value based on the following principles:

- Functional neutrality. Every acquisition is neutral for the functionality of the acquired entity. That is, organizations and institutions are acquired as a whole and post-merger integrations (PMI) do not take place.

- Wealth neutrality. Every acquisition is neutral for the P+L of the respective counterparty of World Inc. That is, the net worth of the counterparty does not change after the acquisition. From the counterparty's perspective, the transaction is an asset swap; the counterparty receives cash and transfers assets to World Inc.
- Market prices. Wealth neutrality implies that World Inc. principally acquires the world economy at market prices. It is assumed that such market prices exist or that the parties may reasonably agree on a transfer price based on standard economic methods and price finding mechanisms. All counterparties agree to sell at this market price. Furthermore, it is implied that foreign exchange standards are applied in international acquisitions involving several currencies. Therefore, purchasing power parity (PPP) is not used for valuation.
- Timelessness. We assume that the entire acquisition process takes place within a logical second, therefore conducted *ceteris paribus.*
- Price neutrality. Timelessness implies that prices are fixed, and markets are liquid. Thus, World Inc.'s activities do not influence prices, and activities of market participants need not be taken into account.
- Accounting rules. Strict commercial accounting rules are applied. Without compromising generality, IFRS framework is chosen for this work.

Following these principles, World Inc. acquires the following entities:

- Private households. World Inc. does not acquire personal items without market value, such as apples and pajamas. However, it acquires all non-financial assets, such as buildings and consumer durables (particularly cars and household durables). Furthermore, it acquires all financial assets, namely, bank accounts, insurance assets, pension assets, and household liabilities from mortgages to credit card debts.

- Listed companies. World Inc. acquires all stocks at market prices and pays the market capitalization for all listed companies.
- Non-listed companies. World Inc. acquires all private businesses and SOEs from their owners at fair market prices.
- Governments. World Inc. acquires all governmental authorities and agencies and consolidates their balance sheets. If the assets have no legal owner or are owned by international or supra-governmental bodies, they are also considered governmental assets.
- Central banks. World Inc. acquires all central banks, including their gold and currency reserves. The last currency is substituted by World Inc.'s equity.

The entire world economy is finally reported in World Inc.'s balance sheet.

3.3   FINANCING MECHANISM AND BALANCE SHEET MECHANICS

We need to ensure that this thought experiment is conductible. First, it needs to be financed.

During its inception at phase 1, World Inc. does not own any assets. Thus, it needs to organize its finances. World Inc. agrees the financing with its central bank, the Last Central Bank. Without compromising the generality, we may assume that the last currency is USD, and the Last Central Bank is the US Federal Reserve System (FED).

How would such a financing mechanism work? The balance sheet of a central bank has currency reserves on the asset side and currency on the liability side. Typical currency reserves include monetary gold, foreign currencies, and securities (e.g., bonds) of high quality by various debtors. The Central Bank accepts these items in return for cash in their currency (see Fig. 2, phase 1). The Last Central Bank agrees to accept World Inc.'s bonds as security for providing the company with the Last Currency (USD).

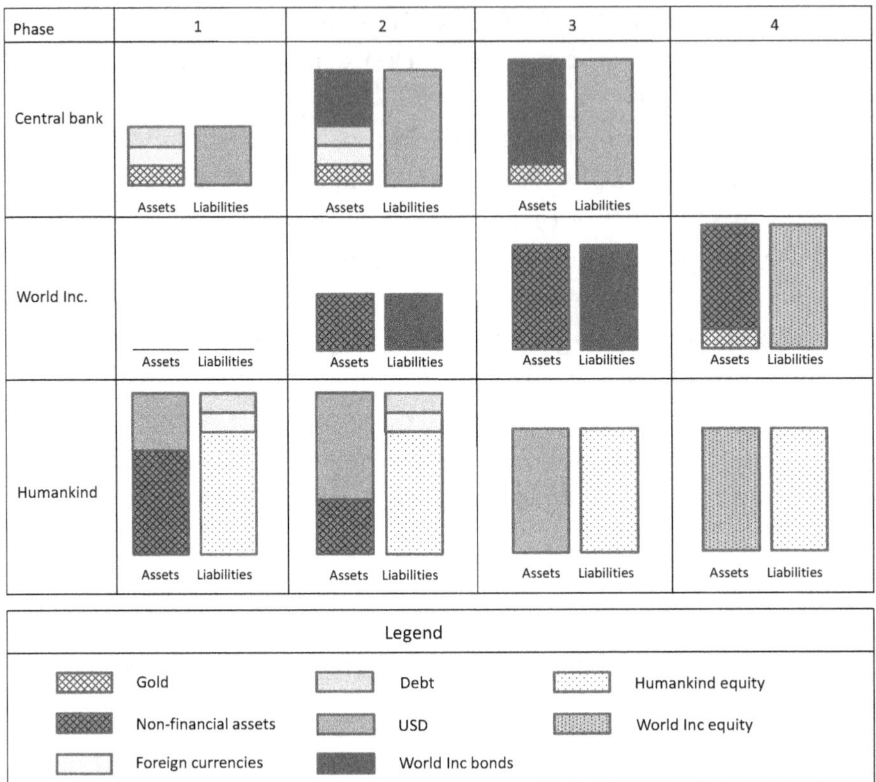

Figure 2:   Acquisition process and balance sheet mechanics

This financing is reasonable from the Central Bank's point of view. Usual debtors of central banks are governmental institutions with high credit rating. However, governmental institutions can also go bankrupt, resulting in defaults of their bonds. In contrast to governmental institutions, World Inc.'s securities are completely asset-backed, World Inc. does not pay prices beyond market value, and controls economically productive resources. World Inc. cannot go bankrupt, as discussed in the following chapters. Thus, its bonds are securities of highest creditworthiness.

We need to assume, however, that the Last Currency is a fiat currency. Because World Inc.'s balance sheet expands considerably during the acquisition process, the same is true for the balance sheet of the Last Central Bank. Thus, the bank needs to create large amounts of the Last Currency. These sums exceed any reasonable sum a commodity currency could provide.

This financing mechanism would have not worked within the Bretton Woods system before 1973. It would also have not worked before 1944 with gold standard currencies as the Central Bank would have been unable to create the necessary amount of money. However, under the current fiat money systems today, the acquisition process can be easily financed as it only leverages standard transactions of central banks in times of quantitative easing.

Fig. 2 illustrates the balance sheet mechanics conceptionally. In Phase 1, World Inc. has no assets, and the Central Bank has its standard balance sheet composition. All non-financial assets of the world are held by different participants in the world economy. To simplify, they are consolidated as the humankind. The humankind also owns the cash provided by the Last Central Bank. As a result, humankind becomes the debtor of the Last Central Bank's currency reserves.

In Phase 2, World Inc. is in full acquisition mode. It acquires assets from the humankind, using its borrowings (in USD) from the Central Bank, which is secured by bonds.

In Phase 3, World Inc. has already acquired all commercial assets and foreign central banks. It now owns all non-financial assets. The foreign currency reserves and securities of all debtors, except World Inc., have been resolved after these acquisitions. All foreign currencies have been replaced by the Last Currency (USD). The Last Central Bank now only has monetary gold and bonds from World Inc. as currency reserves. The humankind owns all cash they received from the sale of all their net assets. Thus, they are debt-free.

Lastly, in phase 4, World Inc. has acquired the Last Central Bank, and its monetary gold has been added to the previously acquired assets. All World Inc.'s bonds now can be resolved, and its liabilities comprise only of all USD liabilities of the Last Central Bank.

Evidently, this is nothing else than World Inc.'s equity. Every USD can now be redefined as World Inc.'s share with a nominal value of 1 USD.

Thus, the humankind's last commercial possession is World Inc.'s equity. The wealth of each household, however, is unchanged, because the amount of World Inc. shares equals the net asset value they had originally at the beginning of the process.

3.4   ASSET CLASSES: MONOVALENT AND BIVALENT ASSETS

Fig. 3 shows asset classes based on the IFRS framework. In commercial business, these asset classes are common. Other commercial accounting frameworks, for example, the US Generally Accepted Accounting Principles (US GAAP), show only minor differences from the IFRS framework.

However, in global economic statistics, multiple lists of asset classes are used. The World Bank, for instance, categorizes produced capital, natural capital, and human capital, as their top-level asset categories (World Bank 2006; Lange, Wodon, and Carey 2018). This accounting treatment is because global economic statistics are mostly derived from national accounting of different countries. They apply the SNA, which defines and categorizes assets with major differences to the IFRS and other commercial accounting frameworks. The entire taxonomies (classification systems) differ. Definitions of taxa (asset classes and asset types) are not identical, similar to the resulting classification tree. Moreover, beyond IFRS and SNA, further accounting systems exist, for example, System of Environmental-Economic Accounting–Central Framework (SEEA-CF). Also, their data are leveraged in this study, which also follow a different taxonomy.

How is this possible? The lists of asset classes are not derived from any economic theory. They are historically grown, differ noticeably by framework and legislation, and have been set up by administrative bodies for various purposes. Traditional commercial accounting dates back to medieval Venice, reflecting the requirement of merchants to count their profits. In contrast, SNA roots from Bretton Woods Conference in 1944, which discussed the interest of nations to measure and align their economic performance, following the Great Depression and World War II.

The unclear theoretical situation regarding the underlying values has been commented by many authors. In this study, we use data and literature from different continents of the economic world. Combining asset definitions from different asset taxonomies and different schools of thought would cause more inaccuracies. Therefore, we apply the following terminology and principles:

- Primarily, IFRS taxonomy is used.
- Top-line IFRS asset categories are called "asset class."
- Sub-categories of asset classes are called "asset type."
- Other asset entities derived from other accounting frameworks (e.g., SNA and SEEA-CF) or used by literature in general terms are called "asset category."
- Widely used asset terms (e.g., "inventories") are written in small caps ("INVENTORIES"), if the term specifically refers to an asset class or asset type in the World Balance Sheet. If the term is less well-defined, it is written in lower case.

Many asset and liability classes shown in Fig. 3 are not reported in World Inc.'s final balance sheet because they offset during the consolidation process due to accounting identities. For example, the face value of an open bill is accounted for as account receivable (asset) of company A and as account payable (liability) by company B. When World Inc. acquires companies A and B, the open bill is resolved during the consolidation process. Thus, at the end of the acquisition process, World Inc. has neither accounts payable nor accounts receivable, in the absence of any other counterparty.

Balance sheet frame (IFRS)		
Assets	**Monovalent**	**Bivalent**
Fixed assets		
Property	X	
Plant	X	
Equipment	X	
Goodwill	X	
Intangible assets	X	
Investments in Financial assets > 1 yr		X
Investments in Associates and JVs		X
Current assets		
Inventories	X	
Prepaid expenses		X
Investments in financial assets <1yr		X
Assets held for sale	n/a	n/a
Accounts receivables < 1 yr		X
Cash and cash equivalent	(X)	X
Liabilities and equity		
Current liabilities		
Accounts payable		X
Current income tax payable		X
Short-term provisions		X
Other current liabilities		X
Non-current liabilities		
Loans payable		X
Issued debt securities		X
Deferred tax liabilities		X
Provisions, e.g. pension obligations		X
Other non-current liabilities		X
Equity		
Paid-in capital	n/a	n/a
Share capital		X
Retained earnings	n/a	n/a
Revaluation reserve	n/a	n/a
Other acc. reserves	n/a	n/a
Non-Controlling Interest	n/a	n/a

Figure 3:   IFRS asset classes

What asset and liability classes offset during the consolidation process? This happens exactly when the accounts exist in two balance sheets and have an opposite normal balance (e.g. on the assets side of company A and the liabilities side of company B).

This phenomenon gives rise to the following definition. An asset is referred to as monovalent when it exists only in one balance sheet (the asset side). In contrast, an asset is referred to as bivalent when it exists in two balance sheets (the asset side of company A and liability side of company B, respectively).

In contrast to asset taxonomies, the feature of an asset being monovalent or bivalent is theoretically founded, and natural. The difference is fundamental and not subject to social or political discourse. It is a real economical feature of an asset, not a political–economical feature.

One economic party can create a monovalent asset. A monovalent asset can be created during a production process. Then, it originates from a producer's balance sheet. It also can be a natural resource, which originates from the balance sheet of a fisherman or miner. Regardless, the asset has intrinsic value and reflects a real economic creation process. It cannot be created *ex nihilo* (out of nothing).

In contrast, two economic parties create a bivalent asset. Bivalent assets are created by contracts between counterparties and therefore through trade. A liability is created and sold to a lender. This process does not generate any intrinsic value. Thus, bivalent assets, reported on the opposite sides of balance sheets and resolving after consolidation, can be created *ex nihilo*.

According to a common definition, a "financial asset" is a liquid asset that is valued based on a contractual right or ownership claim. Although this definition does not refer to balance sheets, it identifies all financial assets as bivalent assets. However, financial monovalent assets exist, for example, monetary gold. Although financial and bivalent assets overlap, they are not identical; our definition is not redundant.

Based on the IFRS asset classification shown in Fig. 3, the following behaviors can describe assets during the process:

- Monovalent assets are acquired once at market prices. They are reported in World Inc.'s final balance sheet in their unmodified asset class.
- Bivalent assets are acquired twice, as asset and liability. They are consolidated during the process. In World Inc.'s balance sheet, the respective asset classes are eliminated. If the remaining value from consolidation is different from zero, this remaining value is accounted for as INTANGIBLE ASSET.
- Some IFRS asset classes are specifically reported because they have informative functions for market participants (e.g., assets held for sale). These terms are not applicable to World Inc. (n/a) as further market participants or counterparties are eliminated. Therefore, these assets are reclassified during the consolidation. They are adequately reported under another asset class.
- CASH AND CASH EQUIVALENTS (money) is a special case. Historically, money was considered a monovalent asset, for example, as gold and silver coins. These money systems are called commodity money systems. However, nowadays, all national currencies are fiat money and thus bivalent (see Chapter 9). After the acquisition of the world's central banks, only the monovalent components of the world's money systems remain in World Inc.'s balance sheet.

Fig. 4 shows the structure of World Inc.'s balance sheet at its conception.

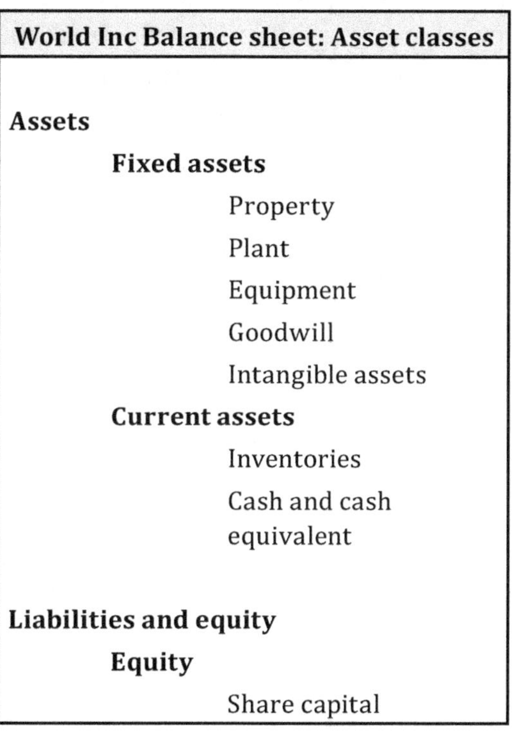

Figure 4:   World Inc. Balance Sheet: Asset classes

3.5   INVARIANCES: INDEPENDENCY AND COMMUTATIVITY

Iterating through the assets of more than 7 billion people or consolidating the balance sheets of approximately 200–300 million companies (following different estimations) is impossible. Statistical information of accumulated asset classes is needed. Thus, invariances in the process described have to be analyzed. What process permutations and transformations let the final World Inc. balance sheet unchanged?

Firstly, all transactions are independent, which means that the result of an acquisition is not dependent on the result of a previous acquisition. This fact is already an implication of the use of the IFRS framework.

Secondly, the process is commutative. What asset we acquire first does not matter. For example, a house can be acquired first and then the company owning such house, or the company and the house can be purchased together. Regardless of the scenario, the house needs to be valued once at market price and integrated in World Inc.'s balance sheet. Similarly, acquiring a liability first and then the asset or vice versa does not matter. Bivalent assets are also consolidated once.

Therefore, World Inc.'s balance sheet can be built by asset class irrespective of the order of the acquisition (outlined in Chapter 3.3.) without compromising the outcome.

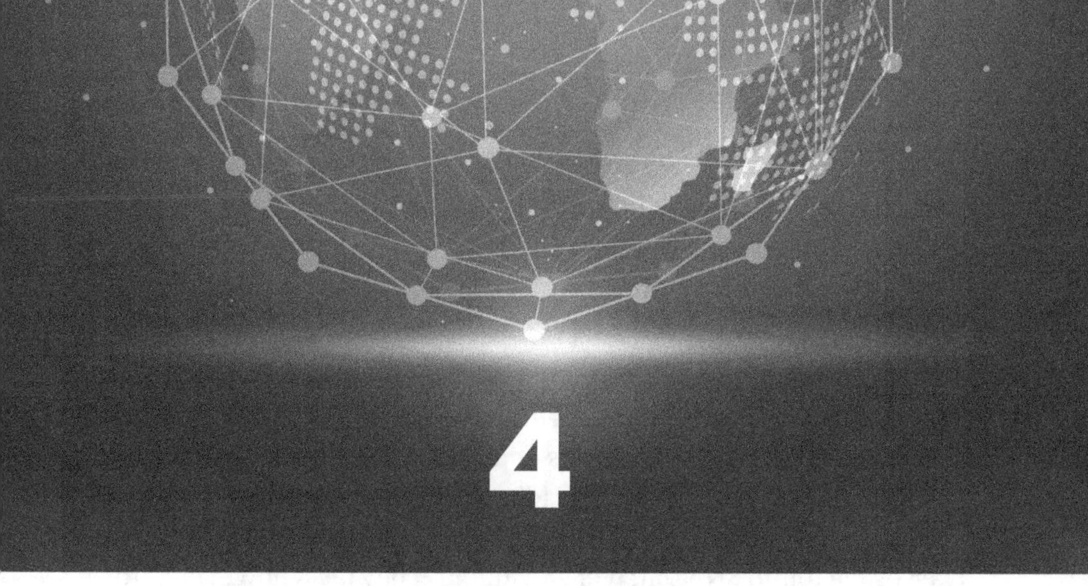

4

Literature Review and Methodology

To our best knowledge, a World Balance Sheet in a true financial accounting logic has not previously been published.

However, this work is only possible through the work of many institutions and authors who have contributed to the data sources, methodology, and theoretical elements, which we have compiled and integrated. During our work, we found that establishing a World Balance Sheet would have been impossible in the past considering the extensive lack of reliable data. During 2016–2018, critical new studies were developed, which contribute to the success of this work. Despite this numerous literatures, data and theory still have certain gaps.

Here, we can only give a brief overview over data provision, frameworks, institutions, and authors, and over critical theoretical elements.

4.1 DATA PROVISION

We utilized more than a hundred data sources for this study. Here, we give a brief overview about the structure of these data sources.

System of National Accounts (SNA)

The backbone of the world's economic data aggregation is the SNA. This framework was established in 1953 and has the most recent release in 2008 (United Nations et al. 2011). It is used as the global accounting system for the world's national economies. SNA data significantly contribute to our study. Particularly for fixed asset classes we found SNA data very valuable. They lack, however, information in other asset categories (e.g., LAND, SUBSOIL ASSETS, INTANGIBLE ASSETS). Therefore, further and specific sources are utilized.

First-tier sources: the World Bank, United Nations, IMF

The usefulness of small data aggregations for the compilation of worldwide data is limited. Completeness, comparability, and standardization are the significant features of these sources that have aggregated global data about the world's capital.

In the first line of these sources are the World Bank (World Bank Data Catalog 2019), UN (United Nations Statistics Division 2019), and IMF (IMF 2019), whose databases are intended to supply the world's decision-makers with economic and political data. The core of their databases is the SNA system, which they maintain, manage, complement, and publish. These sources are considered first-tier for our purposes given their reliability and credibility.

The publications of the World Bank are crucial for this work. The World Bank has published the study "The Changing Wealth of Nations 2018" (Lange, Wodon, and Carey 2018), which gives a global perspective of the world's assets. This study focuses on the changes between 2010 and 2014 and on the elements for ecological policymakers. The World Bank had published precursors of this study (World Bank 2011), the first one in 2006 (World Bank 2006).

In some asset classes (e.g., PROPERTY, FIXED ASSETS, and HUMAN CAPITAL), our work widely follows the World Bank's analyses. However, several asset classes are not taken into account by the World Bank, namely, INTANGIBLE ASSETS, CONSUMER DURABLES, and governmental assets. These assets require data sources beyond the reach of the data integrators of international intergovernmental institutions.

Second-tier sources: Global organizations and think tanks

Several international agencies aggregate their members' detailed economic data in a coalition of the willing. This category includes OECD (OECD Statistics 2019), Eurostat (Eurostat 2019), systematic global databases such as Penn World Tables (Penn World Tables 2019), and the Food and Agriculture Organization of the United Nations (FAO).

Furthermore, organizations beyond the large intergovernmental institutions provide key data. These studies have been provided by various publishers, including large international consulting firms, financial services companies, and think tanks; data are typically compiled from different sources. Although SNA data are leveraged if feasible, other data are primarily employed. Most of the data comes from the financial services industry, its regulators and central banks. These data are used because they are timelier than SNA data and show less differences compared with the IFRS accounting principles. For example, global wealth reports (Brandmeir et al. 2018; CapGemini 2018; Shorrocks 2018; Zakrzewski et al. 2018) allow for analyses of different bivalent asset classes, PROPERTY and CONSUMER DURABLES.

Special examinations about certain asset classes published in the last two years also contribute to this study. These studies focus on INTANGIBLE ASSETS (Haigh et al. 2018) and PENSIONS. Stockholm International Peace Research Institute (SIPRI) also maintains databases with value for this study.

Due to the high reputation of these organizations, editors, and authors the significant contribution of data provided, these sources are considered high-quality second-tier sources. However, compared with first-tier sources, they have two weaknesses. Firstly, they rarely cover the whole globe; typically, only a part of the world is covered (frequently high-income countries). Secondly, they may not completely follow international standards methodologically, which may require adjustments due to their distinct differences.

Third-tier sources: National organizations and specialists

Various specific studies have been utilized to fill data gaps of important countries outside OECD and those not completely covered by global financial markets. Editors differ from governmental institutions to think tanks and non-government organizations (NGOs). We have focused on organizations with a good reputation. Publications of single authors were occasionally used. Thus, these third-tier sources have the least quality as discussed in each chapter.

4.2 NUMERICAL ACCURACY

Numerical accuracy is well-rooted in natural sciences. For example, Cesium (Cs) is a chemical element whose atoms show radiation of a specific frequency (f_{Cs}). This frequency is precisely known and used since 1967 to define a second, i.e., 1 sec = 9,192,631,770/f_{Cs}. This definition shows ten valid digits. In 2019, the accuracy of the ^{133}Cs measurement was improved to fifteen digits. That is, the potential error is less than a millionth of a billionth of the measured frequency. In natural sciences, quantitative data come along with confidence intervals and error bars. Significant work is invested to diminish these error bars in a systematic and transparent manner over time.

In economics the culture is different. For example, in accordance with statistical standards, scientific use, and economic theory, the World Bank publishes the produced capital of Germany as 19,183,999 MUSD in 2014, without giving a confidence interval. This number gives the impression of having eight valid digits. However, are we well-advised to simply use this figure at face value? Unfortunately, not. An analysis of literature indicates that the number of valid digits may be only one and that a reasonable error range of several percentage points exists.

Therefore, we systematically monitor accuracy in this study. We cannot expect the numerical results of this first World Balance Sheet to be completely accurate in every detail, given the complexity of the world's asset landscape. Thus, error sources and their potential impact should be analyzed. Some major drivers of inaccuracy are discussed here in advance, and other specific topics are discussed in the respective chapters.

4.3   THEORETICAL AND PRACTICAL BOUNDARIES OF SNA

The SNA system has certain intrinsic issues that limit its use in general, particularly for the purposes of this work. Thus, SNA data contribute to the overall skeptical assessment of data accuracy.

Limited completeness and timeliness of data

Many SNA data are not available in some countries due to several reasons. For example, these countries either do not have an established strong national statistics agency or have agencies that face data gathering issues. In addition, some countries do not report certain data, though they could. Reporting the value of military weapon systems is demanded by the 2008 SNA. However, numerous countries do not report on these numbers, presumably on the grounds of national security. Moreover, in other asset categories such as PENSIONS, non-performing DEBT, and PROPERTY, lack of transparency is widely practiced.

Considering that global aggregation depends on data availability in (nearly) all countries, only a small part of the SNA accounts is available on a global basis. The UN, World Bank, and IMF report global data when more than 100 countries have reported on those. Therefore, the implementation of SNA framework into statistical practice of the countries deserves some attention. This implementation is not truly enforced. It can take many years from a new release of SNA until a thorough reporting of the majority of countries. Some SNA 2008 report elements have not been successfully implemented to date.

Limited focus on capital stock data

The UN currently reports 27 values of the SNA system as "Main Aggregates" on a global basis (United Nations Statistics Division 2019). These values are comprised of 16 GDP-related, 6 value added-related, and 3 gross national income (GNI) variants. Evidently, GDP measurement is the core purpose of the SNA.

Many authors have criticized the GDP composition and calculation within the SNA framework. Our work does not discuss this topic; unlike the SNA, we focus on asset stocks, not on annual production. Here, however, global data show gaps; that is, the SNA's fixed asset classes are not reported by many countries on a global level. Therefore, they are not part of the 27 first-tier Main Aggregates but are only part of the Main Aggregates and Detailed Tables section of SNA reporting, the second-tier reporting level. Every global consolidation requires models and assumptions to close the gap of missing country information.

However, these data, on which all major studies rely, face serious accuracy issues. In particular, assets are not valued directly. Companies perform physical inventories (stock-taking) to validate their balance sheet positions. This process does not happen in national accounting. The stocks of Fixed Assets are modeled from the Gross Fixed Capital Formation as inflow and a dynamic model for depreciation and outflows. The logic is formulated according to the following (Meinen, Verbiest, and Wolf 1998):

(A)   The net stock of a specific asset in the opening balance sheet plus

(B)   The total value of the assets acquired minus

(C)   The total value of disposed assets minus

(D)   The consumption of fixed capital plus

(E)   Other volume changes (e.g. discovery of subsoil assets [+] natural disasters [–]) plus

(F)   Revaluations,
        is identical to the value of
(G)   The net stock of the asset in the closing balance sheet.

Only (B) is annually reported in the SNA as gross fixed capital formation. All other values have limited data sources and thus need to be modeled. Therefore, extracting final stock values is a modeling task rather than a measurement task. As the Indian economist Datta notes:

> "Measurement of capital stock is a formidable task. Yet, it is one of the most common tasks that economists have to undertake or leave up to the statisticians (doing national income accounting) for lack of alternatives. What is undeniable is that the national accounts statisticians undertake an enormous job to churn out some figures." (Datta 2006, p. 173)

Perpetual inventory method (PIM)

The SNA framework recommends the use of PIM (Perpetual Inventory Method) for modeling purposes. Therefore, this simple and user-friendly method has been used by national statistical institutes for decades.

Several authors have examined the quantitative effect of model variations for values (A)–(F) above. The statistical agency of the Netherlands has shown (Meinen, Verbiest, and Wolf 1998) in detail that plausible variations of service lives, discard patterns and depreciation times, lead to changes in the resulting stock value of 20%–30% for each examined parameter independently. The variation of PIM methodological parameters has a comparable effect. Thus, the outcome is sensitive to minor variations of model assumptions. The underlying stock system examined in the study – the Chemical Industry in The Netherlands – had been understood very well by the statistical agency of The Netherlands. Thus, accuracy estimations could be derived with extraordinarily good quality. In the mainstream work of statistical agencies this high level of accuracy is an exception.

Economists have made several well-founded recommendations to improve PIM (Datta 2006). However, the SNA framework adhered to its PIM standard. Thus, these ideas have no tangible impact, yet. All relevant data sources on types of fixed capital remain on this basis and have inherited inaccuracy sources mentioned above.

GDP expenditure approach: Government and household balance sheets

The most important base information for computing capital stocks is gross fixed capital formation. Already this parameter has significant accuracy issues. It is an element of the expenditure approach of GDP, and therefore is subject to the strengths and weaknesses of this approach.

The expenditure approach follows a macro-economic (Keynesian) logic to differentiate production according to the components of final expenditure. Governmental and household consumption are the major final expenditures beyond the gross capital formation. There is a sharp differentiation between "sectoral" accounting behaviors of governments and households on the one hand, which foremost consume, and companies on the other hand, which produce and contribute to capital formation. This contrasting behavior forms a major assumption of macro-economic theory, driving the SNA accounting results. That is, in SNA, neither governments nor households can build capital.

However, this fundamental assumption does not appropriately reflect of governments' (hypothetical) business accounting behavior. As World Inc. is targeting a governmental institution for acquisition, it may find that this institution would have brand value (e.g., public universities such as the grandes écoles of France), intellectual capital (e.g., the US National Security Agency [NSA]), or market value higher than book value based on private business benchmarks (e.g., public hospitals). The differences between Keynesian governmental consumption approach and commercial capital view on governmental assets is rarely visible, because governments do not primarily use business accounting and specifically balance sheets for their financial management. Chapter 7 will discuss these topics.

Moreover, the expenditure measurement framework does not appropriately reflect a (hypothetical) business accounting behavior of households. As World Inc. targets private households for asset acquisition, it may find that these households regard many purchases they made "for consumption" as assets, such cars, household durables, and other similar goods. These goods are considered assets, including by the Financial Service Industry, and are financed accordingly. Some institutions, such as leasing companies, would list these items as either working capital or fixed capital, therefore as assets. Consequently, a hypothetical household balance sheet would reasonably list them as non-financial capital. Therefore, our study covers household durables as discussed in Chapter 6.

Furthermore, many households are small self-employed producers in traditional, pre-industrialized economies. They may work as part-time peasants, gardeners, and street traders. The SNA's theoretical distinction between "producers" and "private households" is violated by hundreds of millions of people. Thus, they contribute to distorting SNA-reported numbers.

Despite our countermeasures, we perceive that the Keynesian principles of SNA expenditure approach may still affect the accuracy of World Inc.'s balance sheet, particularly in the areas of governmental and household assets.

Gross capital formation and CFA

Finally, the quantitative elements of gross fixed capital formation in the SNA have their sources of inaccuracy (Viet 2011). The matrices connecting the industry production with final expenditures are referred to as the supply and use tables. These tables are recalculated by statistical agencies every five years, where modeling is applied when sufficient data are not available. The major method used is the Commodity Flow Analysis (CFA). Similar to PIM, this method has also been used for decades for its ease of use. One of the oldest and most cited sources for the use of CFA begins with the sentence: "Flow studies have been rightly criticized for their conceptual poverty." (Smith 1970)

Again, the main issue is not the applied modeling method but the absence of reliable primary data. Similar to the supply and use tables, statistical agencies benchmark household's consumption every few years. Intermediate annual numbers are derived via modeling.

The total effect of these auxiliary methods on the resulting data accuracy is impossible to quantify. Nevertheless, the quantitative effect is clearly significant. This arises when a methodological change is applied to a statistical agency's work. Drivers can include updates of the framework (e.g., a new release of SNA accounting) or a change in data gathering or data modeling approach. In many cases, resulting totals jump by several percentage points, sometimes double digit. This phenomenon has been observed by many authors, and examples are cited in this study.

When constant methods are applied, results may look stable every year. However, this only shows that the measurements are precise. Precision means measuring the same result when measuring twice. However, this is not the same thing as accuracy. Accuracy means measuring what we claim to measure. Systematic modeling errors do not impact precision, but they significantly reduce accuracy; we are dependent on the latter.

4.4   BEYOND SNA: DATA GAPS AND THEORETICAL BOUNDARIES

Our work is based on profound data sources as shown in Chapter 4.1. However, data availability and validity in some areas are limited. These topics are discussed in the detailed chapters by asset class. Here, a brief preview is provided:

Immature and unexplored subsoil assets

The accounting standards of raw materials industry favor mature sources of SUBSOIL ASSETS with high specific investments.

Legally and originally, unexplored subsoil resources are government properties. For exploration and exploitation, the state sells licenses to raw material companies. Neither the subsoil resources themselves nor the licenses are reported in any governmental balance sheet. Therefore, government's financial systems do not monitor subsoil resources' asset value appropriately.

Licensed companies also generally do not activate subsoil assets in their balance sheets. Instead, they activate their investments in exploration sites and depreciate them over the years in which the resource is used. The license is only a subordinate position within this investment. Revenue from the resource is recognized only at the time of sale. Thus, the sales potential of the resource does not influence the asset value in accounting but the sunk investment.

Therefore, immature and unexplored resources are undervalued. Consequently, the World Bank observes that the "natural capital per person in high-income countries is three times that in low-income countries, $19,525 versus $6,421 in 2014, even though the share of natural capital in high-income OECD countries is only 3 percent." (Lange, Wodon, and Carey 2018, p. 9). The high balance sheet valuations of mature sources in high-income countries are not in accordance with the allocation of natural resources across the globe. Although some high-income countries own significant subsoil assets, the majority of subsoil resources are located in middle- and low-income countries.

The accounting situation of unexplored resources is also unsatisfactory. Theoretically, each atom of a subsoil resource, such as iron and copper, is a part of the world's raw materials and thus an asset. However, the vast majority of iron and copper atoms are assigned the asset value of zero. Large areas of the globe, for example, submarine areas and arctic regions, are neither explored nor statistically monitored. Therefore, financial data about unexplored natural resources are neither appropriate nor reliable.

In our study, we have decided to follow the usances of national accounting and the raw materials industry and not to assign any asset value to unexplored resources. World Inc. thus can acquire all unexplored subsoil assets for free.

Non-listed companies

World Inc. acquires all companies of the world. Companies are traded with transaction prices higher than their book value, typically. Different intangible assets mark the difference between market capitalization and book value. All companies can acquire goodwill and build brand value and IP. However, qualified data about these various intangible asset classes are only sufficiently available for listed companies.

For non-listed companies, limited data exist. "The vast majority of businesses in the world are privately held; yet, few academic articles aim at computing the market values of those firms." (Gadzinski, Schuller, and Vacchino 2016, p. 14). Most literature focuses on small and medium-sized enterprises (SMEs). This subgroup of companies is not well-standardized as their definition differs across the globe. In the European Union (EU), companies with less than 250 employees are considered SMEs (European Union 2003), provided they stay within certain revenue and balance sheet limits. In China, these limits are different and depend on the industry. Larger companies are included in the definition of SMEs than in the EU. In certain cases, SMEs in China can employ up to 2,000 people. Other countries have also their definitions. Due to this heterogeneity in SMEs' definition, integrating SME data on a global scale becomes a challenge.

Notwithstanding, the majority of global GDP is produced by non-listed companies. After acquiring all these companies, which comprise more than 200 million entities, World Inc. will report significant intangible assets from these acquisitions.

For our study, we have decided to model these asset types based on various heterogeneous sources.

Governmental assets

Commercial balance sheets for governments are not sufficiently created to support our work. The United Nations Conference on Trade and Development (UNCTAD) propagates the Sovereign Asset and Liability Management (SALM) framework (Koc 2014). This framework is based on governmental balance sheets and shall improve nations' asset and liability management. However, the full implementation of SALM cannot be registered anywhere. A recent work of the World Bank (Cangoz, Boitreaud, and Dychala 2018) shows that only a fraction of states creates balance sheets, and that these balance sheets have very specific and generally limited use for financial management of governmental assets. As discussed, the balance sheet elements of the SNA indicate that the implementation of international standards for governmental balance sheets and asset accounting is lagging. This situation is also evident in Europe, where implementation is relatively best.

Literature has overcome to a certain degree the Keynesian view implemented in SNA, that governments consume and cannot build capital. However, the literature focuses on the question whether and how much government spending contributes to economic growth. A recent overview study (Gupta et al. 2014) summarizes the literature since Aschauer (Aschauer 1989, 2000). On average, government spending positively impacts economic growth (output elasticity: 0.15). Government spending is therefore not only consumption, but also creates benefits that promote economic growth.

This focus of literature on economic growth is counterintuitive. Society does not primarily allocate investments to the public sector for the purpose of economic growth. Rather, there is a widespread belief that the private sector is good at driving economic growth on its own. Thus, public spending is allocated to build infrastructure, to improve process reliability (security and law enforcement), and to subsidize public services (basic research, education, health, and pensions). All of these government activities lead to the creation of reasonable values.

However, in accounting, these values remain invisible as the SNA does not report these assets. Furthermore, governments do not set up balance sheets to document them. In addition, no liquid market exists for government agencies and public assets to provide observable and reliable price information similar to company acquisition market.

Nevertheless, there are some levers more advanced asset modeling could use to start from.

Firstly, many government activities and services can be executed also by private companies, for example, private and public hospitals, schools, universities, data centers, and security providers. Based on private companies' commercial information, a benchmark model could be developed. However, this model would be highly theoretical for this study. Thus, our final judgment indicates that reliable data are not sufficient for this approach.

Secondly, from World Inc.'s perspective, the acquired public agencies are comparable to its business infrastructure, such as office footprint, information technology (IT), administration services (finance, human resources, and procurement). Infrastructure is provided to decrease operation costs and improve efficiency. IT standardizes processes, provides information for improved decision making, eliminates errors, and improves efficiency. In addition, administrative services enable standardized, reliable, and effective processes. Thus, from a company's point of view, business infrastructure serves more on profitability objectives and risk management than top-line growth.

The interpretation of governmental assets as World Inc.'s business infrastructure would invite to the modeling of corresponding values. However, similar to private service benchmark approach, we are faced with lack of reliable data and numerous hypothetical elements.

Therefore, we have decided to adhere to the SNA and international reporting standards for this work, despite their shortcomings. For World Inc., this approach implies that it needs to pay only the assets' book value for every public agency. Evidently, this decision entails risk of underestimating governmental assets, particularly governmental intangible assets that are valued at zero.

Canonized discount factors and asset inflation

In natural sciences, natural constants have two sides. In theory, they result from very complex and intellectual theories about various functional models of the world. Practically and numerically, natural constants can be used very easily in calculations to describe the world quantitatively.

Similarly, in economics, certain parameters result from extensive theories on macro- and microeconomic systems. Some of these parameters are used as discount factors in equations of this study. For example:

r is the return rate on capital;

ρ is the time preference rate on consumption; and

d is the time preference rate on work.

These parameters are embedded in theoretical models of capital markets, production functions, and utility functions. Thus, they are considered to be structural long-term economic constants. Hence, they are used in economic models to quantify real economic phenomena in the same way as natural constants. For decades, the same values are assumed in literature and practical statistical work for these parameters.

However, the theoretical and empirical basis for the chosen numerical values tends to be weak. Thus, it can be said that these parameters have been canonized.

For example, a vast majority of studies sets r, the return rate on capital, to 4%. Different uncertain sources are cited for this value. Typical is the World Bank:

> "The 4 percent discount rate is the long-term (100 years or more) real return on financial assets

> globally, derived from Credit Suisse data." (Lange, Wodon, and Carey 2018, p. 223, note 1)

The famous anecdotal long-term study by Credit Suisse is not cited. Thus, let us assume that Credit Suisse has found their long-term average r as exactly 4% (not 3.95% or 4.06%). However, this finding cannot prove that 4% is an appropriate estimation for r in the next 20–25 years.

In retrospect, we know that the return on investment was higher than 4% in the past. Authors of studies about the 18th and 19th century tend to use $r = 6\%$. Evidently, the rate of return on capital is subject to long-term structural developments and, therefore, not a (natural) constant, but a (structural) parameter.

At present, we reasonably assume that we have entered an era of substantially lower returns on capital than in times of Credit Suisse. After the financial crisis in 2008, central banks have started a secular policy of low interest rates, which is expected to continue in the future.

This policy resulted in the rise of asset prices, particularly for real estate and stocks. This phenomenon has been referred to as asset inflation. For some readers, this expression may connote something artificial, temporary, or illusional. However, the rise of asset prices is absolutely real and fundamentally justified as it follows economic laws. Market participants estimate current and future returns on capital lower than the canonized return of 4%. Assets' values are calculated as discounted cash flows. When the return rate on capital r decreases, asset value increases. In the first approximation with simplifying assumptions, the law of error propagation predicts that the relative change in asset value behaves proportional to the (negative) relative change in discount rate. That is, an asset price increases by 1% when the expected discount rate decreases by 1 relative percentage point, as illustrated in the above example from 4% to 3.96%.

Canonized discount parameters are insolvably intermingled in all data sources used in this study. For comparability over time and for global integration, constant prices are constructed and assumed systematically. Furthermore, we perceive that constructing better empirical estimations for discount parameters is impossible.

Therefore, we continue to use canonized parameters according to cited literature and data sources. Nevertheless, we are aware that this factor alone will create a potential accuracy risk of several percentage points for the respective asset classes.

4.5 TWO INDEPENDENT METHODS FOR THE WORLD BALANCE SHEET

One of the functional strengths of business accounting is its nature of double-entry bookkeeping. Balances and accounting identities help find errors and improve reliability. The sum of assets in a balance sheet must equal the sum of liabilities. Liability data quality supports asset data quality.

This functional strength of the balance sheet does not easily work for World Inc. The liability side of its balance sheet is not structured beyond equity. Hence, the bottom–up composition of the asset side is not cross-checked by a corresponding complexity of the liability side. Due to considerable accuracy issues in the sources of many asset classes, this is worrying.

Nevertheless, an independent top–down approach exists. The World Bank has used this approach in their first wealth study "Where is the Wealth of Nations?" (World Bank 2006).

Based on the work of Hamilton and Hartwick (Hamilton and Hartwick 2005), the World Bank sets up a top–down estimation for "total wealth" W. Total wealth is found as the NPV of the humankind's future consumption (World Bank 2006). Although this finding is crucial, it is not necessarily immediately intuitive. Readers are not required to follow Hamilton and Hartwick's concept, neither through the World Bank's reception of it. Later, we will derive the same result through a simpler path. Nevertheless, we provide here the original equations.

Because a continuous time variable is used, the NPV takes the form of an integral Eq. (1a) as follows:

$$W_t = NPV\left(C(t)\right) = \int_t^\infty C(t)\, e^{-\rho(s-t)}\, ds$$

Where

W_t is the total value of wealth or capital in year t;

C(t) is consumption in year t;

ρ is the pure rate of time preference; and

s is the time variable running from year t to ∞.

In accordance with the literature, statistical agencies, and the World Bank, we use a digital time with annual time slices. Under these circumstances, Eq. (1) takes the form of Eq. (1b):

$$W_t = NPV\left(C(t)\right) = \sum_{i=t}^{t+T-1} \frac{C(i)}{(1+\rho)^{i-t}}$$

Here we allow finite consumption time T.

Hamilton and Hartwick made their conclusions after setting up principal equations based on neoclassical theoretical standards and establishing certain assumptions about asset sustainability and simplified production functions. As basis for a statistical global analysis, this approach looks a bit questionable. Consequently, the World Bank validated their equation (World Bank 2006) by statistical evidence, which was presented in a whole chapter of their study. Although correlation coefficients of their regressions only rarely exceed 0.3, the World Bank finally uses this approach to crosscheck their bottom–up asset aggregation.

The World Bank finds a significant higher value for W than for the aggregated sum of assets A. Thus, the identified assets A cannot support the world's known consumption as the shortfall accounts to approximately 78% of total W. This remainder is defined as "Intangible Capital" and cannot be resolved or explained by the World Bank in detail. The World Bank states:

> "The largest share [of the wealth of nations], intangible capital, consists of an amalgam of human capital, governance, and other factors that are difficult to value explicitly." (World Bank 2006, XX, endnote of executive summary).

Given the relatively uncertain neoclassical theoretical basis of their equation, weak statistical evidence, and the resulting unexplained 78% of the world's capital, the World Bank has not pursued this approach further and has not repeated the analysis in their successive studies in 2011 and 2018.

However, the World Bank missed that their Eq. (1) can be independently derived from an accounting identity. This idea gives Eq. (1) a strong basis in commercial accounting, making it immediately evident.

This insight can be derived from an examination of a private balance sheet. Although setting up a household balance sheet is not based on legal and commercial standards, the principles are widely accepted (Looman 2006). A private balance sheet has the following structure (Fig. 5).

Private assets comprise firstly the private commercial assets. These asset classes are illustrated in Fig. 3 — the same non-financial and financial assets every business would report. However, human capital also forms part of private assets. A private person's labor income is a major contributor to wealth and also the most important or sole contributor for many people. HUMAN CAPITAL is calculated as the NPV of labor income.

Private Balance Sheet	
Assets	**Liabilities**
Commercial assets	Commercial liabilities
Human capital (NPV of Work income)	NPV of Consumption
	Equity

Figure 5:   Private Balance Sheet: asset classes

Similarly, private liabilities primarily comprise private commercial liabilities. Because private persons have to secure their life, they additionally need to account for their future consumption. Thus, the NPV of consumption is an important private liability and, in many cases, the most important one.

Private equity is the residual item in the balance sheet, which is transferred by private individuals to their next generations to contribute to their consumption.

Now, an examination of a private balance sheet after World Inc. has acquired all world assets shows that all private assets and liabilities have been transferred to World Inc. Only World Inc. shares remain on the private balance sheet as commercial asset.

A summary of all private balance sheets in one balance sheet of humankind shows the following (Fig. 6):

Balance Sheet of Humankind	
Assets	**Liabilities**
Human capital (NPV of Work income)	NPV of Consumption
World Inc equity	

Figure 6:   Balance sheet of humankind: asset classes

From the accounting identity we find Eq. (2) as follows:

$$W_t = NPV\big(C(t)\big) = A_t + H_t = A_t + NPV\big(w(t)\big)$$

Where

W_t is the total value of wealth or capital in year t,

$C(t)$ is the world's annual consumption in year t,

A_t is the total value of commercial assets (owned by World Inc.) in year t,

H_t is the humankind's human capital in year t, and

w(t) is the humankind's labor income in year *t*.

Thus, the world's total capital can be calculated in two ways. Firstly, in an asset view, all commercial assets A_t and the HUMAN CAPITAL of humankind comprise the world's production factors. Secondly, in a liability perspective, they fund the humankind's CONSUMPTION.

This relationship confirms Eq. (1) from a different and independent theoretical basis. In addition, recent studies have created valuable and substantiated data for HUMAN CAPITAL. Reliable consumption data are provided by Penn World Tables and others. Therefore, Eq. (2) is an independent method of validating data set A_t.

The residual "amalgam" of the World Bank's analysis can now be examined in detail in this study. It consists of HUMAN CAPITAL of the humankind and the non-SNA components of World Inc.'s balance sheet. Particularly, intangible asset types allow a detailed and quantitative understanding of its components.

4.6   FURTHER METHODOLOGICAL DESIGN DECISIONS

Only well-known standard methods are applied, as cited in the respective chapter, to aggregate the asset data. For example, foreign exchange standards are applied to currency standardization. USD (2014) is used as the reporting currency because it eliminates annual fluctuations due to foreign currency effects.

Furthermore, we use trillion USD (tn USD) as the unit of reporting. Considering its size (1 trillion=1,000 billion), this unit is not very common in economic statistics. To compare, one tn USD approximately equals the value of the world's largest corporations (e.g., Apple and Microsoft [2018]). Indonesia and the Netherlands have been the world's 16th and 17th largest economies in 2018, with approximately 1 tn USD GDP, respectively.

Most recent numbers are based on different years. Many asset classes are reported promptly and data are from recent years (2018 onward), whereas some others are older. Particularly, the SNA figures need time for aggregation. The World Bank's 2018 study refers 2014 data. Similarly, the oldest numbers in our study (e.g., private household durable assets) are from 2014.

To integrate these numbers, we had to either use 2014 as safe reporting year and discard more recent information or renormalize some data to 2018 based on certain limited modeling. We chose to renormalize data to the year 2018 to utilize most recent information. The accuracy risk of this approach is negligible compared with that of the underlying data, as described earlier in this section.

5

Property

5.1 PROPERTY: ACCOUNTING PRINCIPLES

World Inc. accounts for all acquired LAND and all its associated natural resources as PROPERTY. Estimating this asset class is difficult.

Firstly, the SNA does not trace property values. That is, that neither national accounting agencies nor international data aggregators, such as the World Bank, IMF, UN, and other intergovernmental institutions, maintain a standardized and comparable database of property and property values.

Secondly, land ownership in different countries entails various legal differences that alter the respective value. International comparisons are difficult and methodologically impossible in certain circumstances. A worldwide analysis therefore needs to be conducted country by country, which requires significant effort and creates accuracy risks.

Furthermore, land ownership is highly scattered. Only a small fraction is owned by private companies and disclosed in their balance sheets. A large portion is owned by governments and private individuals. These lands are rarely traded, and their values are undocumented. Large swathes of land, for example, the Antarctica and sea grounds, have no clear owner or are explicitly excluded from an ownership principle by international contracts. Thus, land value cannot be aggregated based on balance sheet entries or land charge registers.

To address the issue on land valuation, a value-based approach is applied, following a benchmark approach. Land is used economically to provide services that generate rents annually. To generate this rent income, alternatively to buying land, a certain capital could be invested, yielding an average return rate on capital. This capital is the NPV of the rent income and therefore economically equals the land's value.

Nevertheless, it is noteworthy that different types of land cover provide varied services, economic uses, and therefore different rents.

The World Bank follows this approach in their extensive study on the "The Changing Wealth of Nations" in 2018 (Lange, Wodon, and Carey 2018). Based on a thorough country-level analysis, the World Bank has derived total global values for various PROPERTY types in 2014.

The World Bank calculated the asset value of each PROPERTY type as the NPV of the expected future rents as shown by Eq. (3) below:

$$V = \sum_{i=t}^{t+T-1} \frac{R_g}{(1+r)^{i-t}}$$

Where

V is the value of the PROPERTY type.

R_g is the lagged, five-year moving average of rents in year t-4...t. Using the moving average technique eliminates short-term fluctuations in prices and volumes.

r is the return rate on capital, which is set to 4% as cited in the World Bank's studies.

T is the lifetime of the service. In certain instances, natural resources are depleted, and land covers are changed. These phenomena need to be reflected in finite lifetimes.

Rent drivers vary with the service provided by the PROPERTY involved. Therefore, different variants of Eq. (3) are applied.

We have reviewed the World Bank's approach and follow it in major parts of this study. However, for few land types, particularly for forests, we deviate from the World Bank's approach in detail because the World Bank employs the SEEA-CF (United Nations 2019). This accounting framework was introduced in 2012 as an extension of the SNA and deals with the national accounting of natural resources and renewable energy. Thus, it is valuable for policy advisory and ecologic decision making. Because it differs significantly from IFRS, its value for this study is limited. Based on a critical review of the results of the World Bank's 2014 data, we project 2018 values according to global production and output statistics.

5.2 LAND

LAND is differentiated into seven economic land types, which provide different services and rents as shown in Fig. 7 below:

Land type	Service
Cropland	Crop
Pasture land	Lifestock breeding
Forest	Timber, Non-Wood Forest Products (NWFP)
Barren land	none
Protected areas	none
Urban land	Carries structures
Sea	Fish

Figure 7:   Land types

For each LAND type, one to two standard services are assumed, on which rents are calculated and from which asset values are derived. Services not considered as standard are excluded due to lack of specialized data and limited relevance. These nonstandard services include those related to tourism, renewable energy (e.g., wind, solar), and water supply.

Nevertheless, this design does not imply that World Inc. acquires all sources of water supply or tourism for free. It has to purchase all companies driving these businesses at fair market price. However, if non-private LAND contributes to these businesses, then these LAND types have no special value. For example, the Swiss alps may be assumed to contribute to Switzerland's tourism value of skiing. However, this study rates these mountains as barren land. No explicit tourism value is assigned to them.

Although this approach generates a certain risk of LAND value underestimation, other factors are in the opposite direction. Particularly, the impact of pollution, degradation, and salinization cannot be completely reflected. Although some land areas are severely affected by these factors, their effects cannot be reliably included due to lack of detailed data.

Furthermore, even more complex ecological advantages of land cannot be measured yet. These potential advantages may include water and soil retention, cooling, carbon storage, and wind modification, which are not covered by the SEEA-CF. More work of the international community is required to establish commercially viable measurements of ecological rents.

This approach allows us to evaluate LAND value with known economic use according to LAND type. However, this economic use only partially correlates to physical land cover, resulting in another challenge.

The physical land cover is relatively well-known from satellite observation programs (e.g., Moderate Resolution Imaging Spectroradiometer [MODIS], CCI-LC) monitored by FAO and other international organizations. These satellite programs can track all changes and developments in land cover. For example, changes of forests are visible real-time, as well as natural disasters, drought, and salinization that destroy agricultural lands.

Furthermore, FAO satellite programs are optimized to recognize the economic use of land cover, which helps to generate volume estimations for land types covered in this study. Fig. 8 shows land types derived from MODIS satellite data of FAO (FAOSTAT 2019).

Still, there are caveats.

Firstly, the world's total land area is 149.4 million km^2, which is more than the reported 127.3 million km^2. Although FAO and MODIS may track all lands with economic value (e.g., vegetation), they cannot track 100% of the world's land. Thus, FAO includes and aggregates the information of their member states that do not report in all cases. Technical matters also add to this concern, particularly satellite resolution and quality, which depend on observation angle.

Land type	MODIS coverage type	2014	2017	2018 est
Urban land	Artificial surfaces	781,470	791,830	795,314
Cropland	Herbaceous crop	12,351,930	12,398,960	12,414,676
	Woody crops	1,315,750	1,301,900	1,297,316
Pasture land	Grassland	30,731,010	30,657,100	30,632,503
Forest	Tree covered areas	49,307,080	49,060,390	48,978,435
Barren land	Shrub-covered areas	13,600,710	13,577,410	13,569,652
	Permanent snow and glaciers	14,459,620	14,489,530	14,499,514
	Inland water	2,502,200	2,491,590	2,488,063
	Other	2,295,186	2,585,931	2,667,747
Total land (sqkm)		127,344,956	127,354,641	127,343,220

Figure 8:   Land and coverage types, 2014–2018

Furthermore, not all areas with certain coverage are utilized. That is, lack of population and logistical area access can prohibit economic use. For example, some forests are cultivated, whereas others are not, which cannot be observed by satellites. The value of two parcels of land can also vary significantly regardless of being situated in the same country and having the same land cover.

Agriculture: cropland and pasture land

Agricultural land is conceptually divided into CROPLAND and PASTURE LAND, which are used for crops and livestock, respectively (see Fig. 7). Ecological services are not covered by agricultural land in this study.

Assumptions for the future development of rents need to be made, particularly with regard to volume. Which production rates can be achieved in the future from a given acre of agricultural land? In accordance with the World Bank, we consider foreseeable increases in agricultural productivity, which are extrapolated from long-term observations and projections.

Thus, Eq. (3) is modified into Eq. (4) for both types of agricultural uses as follows:

$$V = \sum_{i=t}^{t+T-1} \frac{R_g}{\left(1+r^*\right)^{i-t}}$$

Where $r^* = r - p_{nm}$;

r is the rate of return on capital set to 4% as discussed above; and

p_{nm} is the annual productivity increase of use n and country m.

For CROPLAND, p is set to 1.94% for all low- and middle-income countries and to 0.97% for all high-income countries, respectively. Accordingly, for PASTURE LAND, p is set to 2.95% for low- and middle-income countries and to 0.89% for high-income countries, respectively.

Evidently, these values are relatively rough approximations of p_{nm}. The source is one of the fundamental papers of the International Food Policy Research Institute (IFPRI), which developed the International Model for Policy Analysis of Agricultural Commodities and Trade (IMPACT). The methodology derived from a fundamental study (Rosegrant, Agcaoili-Sombilla, and Nicostrato 1995) has been used in all World Bank wealth studies since 2006, without changes.

Such changes would be in principle possible because IFPRI has developed IMPACT further (IFPRI 2019). As a result, the intellectual framework (Rosegrant et al. 2008) has become highly complex. Using it for accounting purposes would require significant resources and assumptions about missing data. Therefore, we follow the World Bank's decision to not overcomplicate the analysis, but to adopt the 1995 long-term productivity projections. Empirically, most of these projections have been met reasonably well in the past. This decision has further the advantage of easier comparability of agriculture-related asset values over time.

Based on good FAO statistics about crop and livestock production, the World Bank derived from their groundbreaking study reliable figures for CROPLAND and PASTURE LAND value, respectively. In 2014, according to the World Bank, the global value of CROPLAND accrued to 25.90 tn USD, whereas PASTURE LAND accounted for 13.99 tn USD.

To model the 2018 values from the World Bank's results in 2014, we assume that prices and margins are held constant on 2014 levels. From 2014 to 2018, total CROPLAND has grown by 0.3% as shown in Fig. 8.

The productivity model is more complex. International integration of 2015–2018 crop data has not yet been completed by the World Bank and UN agencies to a global production index. However, detailed production data until 2018 and outlooks for many countries and agricultural commodities are available.

OECD and FAO provide the OECD-FAO Agricultural Outlook for OECD countries. We use these data for our analysis. OECD crop production index has been correlated well with the world crop production index in 2004–2014. However, we have to consider that the productivity growth of the OECD countries during 2004–2014 has reached 36.4% only of the world's average. As correctly predicted in 1995, CROPLAND productivity growth is more rapid in middle- and low-income countries.

This finding allows us to model the crop productivity development on a global level based on the seven most important crops in OECD countries, namely, wheat, maize, rice, other coarse grains, soybean, other oilseeds, and cotton, in the terminology of the FAO.

We find that the yield growth during 2004–2014 has not been achieved in subsequent years. Whereas limited growth was evident between 2014 and 2016, we observe a decreasing productivity rate afterwards. For wheat, rice, other coarse grains, other oilseeds, and cotton, yields in OECD countries have decreased between 2016 and 2018.

In total, the global productivity growth per hectare between 2014 and 2018 for cropland is approximately 1.9%, averaging to 0.47% only annually. Simultaneously, the total cropland has slightly expanded by 0.3% as shown in Fig. 8. Thus, the estimate total value of CROPLAND in 2018 is 26.45 tn USD, averaging to 1.93 million USD/km^2.

For PASTURE LAND, we proceed comparably. To model the 2018 values, we assume that prices and margins remain constant on 2014 levels.

The relationship between PASTURE LAND and livestock production is more complex due to different production types of livestock. E.g., livestock can be raised through nomadic pastoralism in free pasture land, combined farms, and horticulture. "Farming of crops and livestock cannot be considered independent of one another nor should they be considered in isolation." (Robinson 2011, p. 17).

Therefore, we have decided not to apply changes in pasture land in our model.

Instead, we model directly along the production data, which are provided in good quality by OECD-FAO Agricultural Outlook. Five major livestock products are used, namely, beef and veal, pork, poultry meat, sheep meat, and milk. In contrast to crop production, meat production has increased by 5.6% in OECD countries between 2014 and 2018. However, similar to crops, OECD livestock production growth is not representative of the whole world. Between 2004 and 2014, OECD countries have reached 37.6% only of global average growth rate, with good overall annual correlation.

Therefore, the estimated global livestock production growth between 2014 and 2018 is 14.8%, averaging to 3.5% annually. This finding is further accelerated compared with the noticeable growth in previous years. Given that this value stream is assigned to PASTURE LAND, the value of PASTURE LAND in 2018 has increased to 16.06 tn USD, averaging to 524,500 USD/km^2.

Livestock on pasture lands is included in this figure. Livestock is subject to SNA reporting as cultivated biological resources. The SEEA clarifies SNA's definition of cultivated biological resources as "livestock for breeding, dairy, draught, etc. and vineyards, orchards, and other trees yielding repeat products whose natural growth and/or regeneration is under the direct control, responsibility, and management of institutional units." (United Nations et al. 2003, p. 254, para 7.57)

This asset type is listed as "Biological" in Fig. 10 and accrues approximately 0.10% of the world's produced capital, which would translate to 340 bn USD only. However, the SNA reporting about cultivated biological resources does not meet the quality standards of this study. The majority of countries, including the US, do not report on this parameter, and the differences between countries are huge. Therefore, the world's livestock value cannot be separately validated based on SNA sources.

Forest

FOREST is considered a in principle inexhaustible resource given its unlimited lifetime if managed carefully and sustainably. The most important value driver for forest is timber.

Therefore, T in Eq. (3) is ∞ in all forests, where timber production is less than growth rate. Moreover, overexploited forests have finite lifetime, and public and private forests do not differ.

FAOSTAT (FAOSTAT 2019) traces timber production, export prices, and forest lifetimes based on the Global Forest Resources Assessment. Based on these statistics and country-level analysis, the World Bank estimated the timber-related value for all forests to be approximately 2.40 tn USD in 2014.

However, changes between 2014 and 2018 need to be considered.

Firstly, there is a visible tendency to forest depletion. In many countries, particularly in tropical regions, forests are cleared or burned and converted to agricultural land. Nevertheless, forests grow in other areas due to global warming. They expand to previously cold areas. In arid regions forestation also happens. To trace the net effect closely, we leverage the satellite-driven MODIS program (Fig. 9), which is timelier and more accurate than ex-post statistical aggregations. Between 2014 and 2018, total forest area has declined by 0.67%. Because cleared forests tend to be mature and new forests consist of new and small trees, total wood substance has reasonably deteriorated even faster than the forest area.

Moreover, forests' timber value declines. The World Bank had observed stagnant or falling forest timber-related values before 2014. This trend has continued or accelerated. According to the FAOSTAT, the timber production value has significantly decreased since 2014. This finding is partly also a price effect due to large volumes of cleared wood entering the market. Therefore, total timber-related value of the world's forests has further declined. This value is projected to be 1.83 tn USD only in 2018, which is 23.7% less than in 2014.

Compared with other land types, the value of FOREST based on timber production is small. Large parts of the world's forests are not cultivated or only partially economically exploited. This condition and the continuous decline in FOREST value per km^2 have incentivized and accelerated forest burning and clearing, which increased public and political attention. In addition to their direct economic value, forests serve many ecological purposes. Thus, many authors are motivated to quantify forests' ecological benefits beyond timber, which is referred to as non-timber value.

Based on an extensive study (Siikamäki, Santiago-Avila, and Vail 2015), the World Bank has decided to assign significant non-timber value to forests, in addition to the regular timber value. The total non-timber value turns out to be three times the regular timber value. However, we can only partly follow this approach in this study due to several reasons.

The cited study is a meta-analysis of 139 forest studies, introducing 282 value estimates. Fig. 9 gives an overview of the services examined and the value contribution to total non-timber value.

Firstly, these services and their classes are not standardized as they are not covered by the SEEA-CF framework. We are not yet in statistical, but in scientific territory.

Relatively best defined are biological products beyond timber, the so-called Non-Wood Forest Products (NWFP). NWFP include products used as food and food additives. These can be edible nuts, mushrooms, fruits, herbs, spices and condiments, aromatic plants, and game. Further NWFP products are fibers, resins, gums, finally plant and animal products used for medicinal, cosmetic or cultural purposes. But despite the long list of specified products, a final common definition of NWFP has not been established.

The intangible ecological service classes are even less standardized.

Secondly, this disadvantage becomes evident when studying value outcomes. Values per ecological service differ by several magnitudes, not only by country but also by study. The standard deviation of the total value per hectare is 3.8 times the mean value. For accuracy, this volatility is considered extremely high.

Service class	Subservice	Value %
Non-Wood Forest Products	Non-Wood Forest Products	10.8
Recreation	Hunting Fishing Recreation	13.1
Habitat/species protection	Landscape aestethics Cultural existence Habitat protection	24.3
Water services	Water quality Water quantity Hydropower Erosion control Flood protection	51.7
Excluded services	Nutrient cycling Bioprospecting Fuelwood	0

Figure 9:   Non-timber forest services

Thirdly, overlapping and double counting issues exist. Some services do not necessarily depend on the forest cover but on mere existence of an area. For example, water services depend more on the level of precipitation than on the forests that cover the area. However, water and other ecological services are not considered for the other land types. An inclusion only for forests would distort the relative value relation between different land types.

Lastly, only NWFP values are mainly derived from market prices (87%) unlike other ecological services whose values are derived from contingent valuations or opportunity cost comparisons. For example, the water supply is modeled hypothetically for a landscape with no forest. The finding may be that water production may lessen and water would be more expensive or difficult to provide. The difference in value is then accounted for as forest value.

The study of Siikamäki et al. may be well founded ecologically and politically. However, its view conflicts with the IFRS standards. Hypothetic, but unreal value flows must not be activated.

Therefore, we cannot include ecological service classes in our study. Nevertheless, we include the NWFP service class because it completes forests' economical view as source of biological products.

Finally, we find that NWFP accounts for 0.87 tn USD in 2018, approximately 50% of the timber-driven value. Thus, we find that the total value of the world's forests is 2.69 tn USD, averaging to 54,900 USD/km^2 only.

Barren land

Large parts of the globe comprise barren land, namely, deserts, glaciers, mountains, and other unattractive coverages, that meet the following criteria:

- No trading market for this land exists.
- The land is not activated in public balance sheets.
- The land has no regular use or economically valuable services.

LAND that meet these criteria is called BARREN LAND in this study. The World Bank has not examined this land type in their wealth studies but has assigned a value of zero without detailed discussion.

However, assigning this value to barren land means that World Inc. could acquire more than 30 million km^2 land for free, an area equal to the size of Africa. This concept is counterintuitive because unexplored natural resources can have future economic uses that are to be discovered or developed. Moreover, a lower threshold for a value should be established theoretically. The right of ownership includes the right to refuse access and use to other people. This right should have a positive value.

However, recommending distinct values different from zero is difficult due to lack of data and literature. We are limited to the IFRS and commercial accounting principles. Thus, in the absence of a trading value and sources of rent, second-tier commercial methods are employed to derive commercial values.

Firstly, we use a benchmark approach.

The purchase of Alaska by the US in 1867 is a well-known example of BARREN LAND trade. During this time, the entire land of Alaska can be assumed to have met the criteria of barren land. New-York Tribune called the new territory "frozen wilderness." Fur animals, which had formed the major economic value source before 1867, were nearly extinct. The end of this industry had been a major driver of the Russians' willingness to sell Alaska. They could not materialize and exploit alternative land rents. Alaska's total area of 1,518,800 km^2 was sold for 7.6 million USD. When converted to the purchasing power of USD in 2014 (MeasuringWorth.com 2019), this amount would translate to 14.98 bn USD or 9,863 USD 2014/km^2.

Certain data points support the view that the price may have been lower than the fair market price. First, Russia sold Alaska due to the risk of losing the country to England, which owned Canada during that time. For similar reasons, England refused to make a competitive offer.

However, from today's perspective, buying Alaska was not necessarily an economic bargain. Several economists have questioned recently whether the US has obtained positive financial return from their investment. Therefore, would 9,863 USD mark an appropriate benchmark for a value per km^2 of barren land? In any case, it could serve as a lower threshold.

Further data points for prices of barren land are available. Low-priced deserts, which still are considered as agricultural land, have a limited market in certain countries, such as the US, Australia, Morocco, and other arid places. Prices are anecdotal, and price ranges vary widely between 39,000 USD/km^2 (desert-like US) and

200,000 USD/km^2 in outback Australia. These places have agricultural use and minimal infrastructure and logistical access. This condition makes them potentially more attractive than true barren land. Furthermore, real estate prices are generally lower in many countries than in the US or Australia. Thus, these values may mark upper thresholds for a global average price for barren land.

Furthermore, we have considered a probabilistic stance in our analysis, where we found the following global average values per km^2 for LAND types:

- FOREST: 54,900 USD
- CROPLAND: 1.93 MUSD
- PASTURE LAND: 524,500 USD
- Average SUBSOIL ASSETS: 407,800 USD

The lifetime of barren lands is unlimited. That is, T in Eq. (3) is ∞. With r = 4%, 44.2% of the value of barren land comes from the distant future beyond the next 20 years. A 5% chance of converting the barren land after 20 years either into croplands or pasture lands would add 42,650 USD or 11,590 USD, respectively, to the value of barren land. A 5% chance of finding the global average of subsoil resources within 20 years would add 9,012 USD to the value of barren land.

Under these circumstances, assignment of the value of zero to BARREN LAND is unreasonable. Thus, we assigned BARREN LAND a balanced mean between benchmarks and probabilistic values, that is, a global average value of 30,000 USD/km^2. As a result, World Inc. pays 1.00 tn USD for 33.3 million km^2 (Fig. 8) barren land.

Protected areas

According to the World Bank, 14.73% of the world's land area is protected areas (excluding marine protected areas), with a strong progression in the last decades. This area has significantly increased to 18.76 million km^2 in 2018.

However, unlike other land types, protected areas are not defined by their land cover or their sources of economic value. They have heterogeneous cover and are unified by governmental limitations for economic use. In addition to economic uses, ecological benefits also exist. However, assessing these benefits is more difficult than analyzing those of the forests. Due to lack of plausible studies and data, the World Bank decided to assign an opportunity-based value to protected areas, that is, the lower of the local value of either CROPLAND or PASTURE LAND.

However, these land types are the most valuable land types next to URBAN LAND. Therefore, the resulting value is comparably high (415,200 USD/km^2), and for several reasons we cannot follow this approach.

Firstly, protected areas tend to be barren land. Protection has begun in the 19th century, but the majority of protections took place in the 20th century and more recently. Such areas have small population and less cultivation. Thus, they have been protected to preserve natural. That is, these areas had proven to be difficult to exploit and had not disclosed major rent streams. Therefore, assuming that they could alternatively be used as pasture land or cropland is unreasonable. On the contrary, the status of a protected area ensures that commercialization is strictly limited and that agriculture, mining and animal husbandry are restricted.

Where commercialization is possible, the protection can entail large opportunity costs. Police and rangers may need to prevent poaching or limit other inappropriate economic value creation.

In more general terms, protected areas are typically designed as non-profit areas. Applying Eq. (3), these areas would be assigned the value of zero. World Inc. needs to follow the principle of functional neutrality that prohibits altering the legal and commercial status quo. So, would be World Inc. ready to pay a lot for these protected areas?

In our view, assigning the value of zero to protected areas is more reasonable than to barren land. Future value streams are difficult to generate. However, the protected area status is subject to future decision making. Therefore, the generation of future rents is in principle possible, for example, through tourism.

We have decided to assign the value of the respective coverage type to protected areas. Thus, we assign the value of CROPLAND for protected cropland, the value of PASTURE LAND for protected pasture land, and the value of BARREN LAND for protected barren land. These values are less than the World Bank's computations, though the numbers are still significant. The status of protected area does not infringe the value. Therefore, we do not account for an independent asset category of protected areas.

Urban land

Urban land covers only a fraction of the Earth's surface. However, it is the most valuable land type, accounting for more than half of the world's total LAND value. Despite its high value, which drives broad public discussions, the documentation of urban land's value is the weakest of all land types.

As previously mentioned, land value is not traced neither by SNA nor international data integrators. Furthermore, significant legal differences exist between countries, impacting global value aggregations.

Urban land does not provide a specific service. It is merely an infrastructural requirement for buildings and other fixed assets erected on the land. This makes it impossible to use the approach used for all other land types, based on Eq. (3).

The lack of data is contrary to the good and solid state of theory and literature. Value drivers of urban land are well understood (El-Barmelgy et al. 2014). The fundamental bid rent theory is already old; it was introduced in 1826 by Johann Heinrich von Thünen and later integrated in the work of David Ricardo. The theory stipulates that the maximum rent of a parcel of urban land can be derived in a theoretical auction, where the highest bid stipulates the price. The tradeoffs between land price, transportation cost, and space requirement define the market. The model still works with good evidence; the prices are highest in the city center, and typical clusters of commercial and residential use arise. Recent developments have driven the theoretical understanding further. However, this concept does not contribute to our study. The variables of urban value theory are not traced statistically. Real estate statistics are typically limited to single countries or specific building types. However, they relate partly to buildings and partly to land. Therefore, real estate market prices reflect combined land and building prices, which blurs the difference between PROPERTY and PLANT asset classes.

Direct methods to derive urban land values on a larger scale have been employed. One potential source are insurance values. However, insurances typically cover whole buildings, and premiums are based on the buildings' value rather than land value. In addition, direct surveys with public authorities handling urban land have been conducted. However, public authorities tend to handle real estate matters on local municipality level. When central governments deal with urban land, for example, for ground taxes, they rarely have data about market values, and ground taxes have proven incoherent to allow integration. Therefore, these direct approaches have not led to tangible success at present.

Detailed country-level analyses have not been conducted due to lack of successful global integration approach; only relatively rough estimations are available.

The World Bank refers in their wealth analyses to one of their first fundamental papers before starting the wealth accounting studies (Kunte et al. 1998). In this study, the authors recommend to derive URBAN LAND value from the total produced asset value as a percentage. This approach confirms the concept that urban land is an infrastructural precondition for fixed assets.

Thus, the authors recommend Eq. (5) as follows:

$$U = s \cdot u \cdot p$$

Where

U is the value of urban land;

s is the share of structures in all produced assets. The SNA refers the term "structure" to all buildings (dwellings and commercial buildings) and civil engineering infrastructures, such as canals, tunnels, and roads.

u is the share of urban land in the structures;

p is the value of produced assets.

Empirically, the authors found s and u to be 0.72 and 0.33, respectively. The World Bank combines the two factors to 0.24, which results in Eq. (6) as follows:

$$U = 0.24 \cdot p$$

The World Bank uses this equation in their studies.

However, this practical equation with the simple coefficient 0.24 has a questionable basis and is more anecdotal than scientifically well founded.

Moreover, the basis for the estimation of u = 0.33 is relatively weak. The study derives the figure solely from the circumstances in Canada, which had been examined extensively. Although the Canadian real estate market may not be representative of the world, this anecdotal value has been projected to a global level due to lack of differentiated data.

In the absence of better alternatives, the World Bank has urban land value in 2014 based on the simple approach in Eq. (6), in which accuracy risk is high.

Improving this approach to project urban land value in 2018 poses challenges. We will strive to improve the Word Bank's approach by leveraging an improved data situation.

The logic of handling urban land as an infrastructure for buildings requires proportionality to the value of buildings. Other produced assets, such as machinery, equipment, and inventories, have no evident relationship to urban land. That is, we can rewrite Eq. (5) to Eq. (7) to show the true linearity:

$$U = u \cdot B = u \cdot (s \cdot p)$$

Where

B is the value of buildings ("plant" in commercial accounting terms, "structures" in SNA terminology).

Fortunately, better estimations for B exist compared with 1998 (Kunte et al. 1998). Proportions of the world's produced assets can be derived from international databases. Therefore, the 1998 anecdotal estimation for s at 0.72 can improve through statistical evidence.

Detailed data about the composition of produced capital are available for a restricted number of countries. Based on OECD statistics, we set up a list of 21 OECD countries with detailed data from 2017 and 2016 (Fig. 10). These countries include Australia, Belgium, Canada, France, Greece, Hungary, Israel, Italy, Japan, Korea, Latvia, Lithuania, the Netherlands, New Zealand, Poland, Portugal, Slovak Republic, Slovenia, Sweden, the United Kingdom, and the US. They represent 48.8% of the world's total GDP in 2018.

Based on Kunte's definition, we define s as the sum of DWELLINGS and OTHER BUILDINGS in relation to total produced assets. This value varies slightly across the 21 countries examined. Sweden has the lowest value (68.1%), whereas Canada has the highest (82.4%). A systematic dependency of parameter s of the respective country's relative wealth cannot be stated, which allows us to project it to the global level. The GDP-weighted average for all s_i in this sample is 76.4% (Fig. 10). Therefore, we substitute the old 1998 value of s (0.72) with this more reliable and timely value, $s_{new} = 0.764$.

However, we could not find better data or improvement in approach in determining the value of u. The few significant analyzes and publications indicate Kunte's value of $u = 0.33$. Without a viable alternative, we are compelled to follow these analyses' approach.

As we will discuss in Chapter 6.2, we prefer Penn World Table (PWT) 6.1 as the best source for produced capital. Based on this source and Eq. (7), we find the value of the world's URBAN LAND in 2018 at 85.89 tn USD, which averages to 107.99 USD/m^2.

This value is burdened with significant accuracy risk attributable to u as previously discussed. Furthermore, price developments may not be appropriately reflected as the SNA focuses on production. Thus, construction of new buildings and maintenance efforts of real estate are accounted for, but value increases due to increases in the assets' market price may not be reliably traced. Implementation of comprehensive revaluations by statistical agencies lags, despite being theoretically requested by the SNA standards. For example, significant increases in property prices between 2014 and 2018 may be reflected insufficiently.

This skeptical view is supported through cross-checking. According to PWT, produced assets have increased by 16.7% globally between 2014 and 2018 (in real terms). A total of 76.4% of produced assets are buildings. This robust growth exceeded slightly the real GDP growth of 12.1% during the same period. This finding reflects the strong activity of construction industry and investments into infrastructure.

However, real estate price development is already in the same order of magnitude. The Bank for International Settlement (BIS) provides international real estate price indices for residential and commercial properties on behalf of the G20 since 2009 (Bank for International Settlement 2019). The objective is to provide internationally comparable and real-term indices for properties. The different sources of these statistics are still not completely harmonized because quality differs and BIS publishes the data with caveats (Scatigna, Szemere, and Tsatsaronis 2014).

For residential properties, we have evaluated the BIS data of the world's most important 59 economies, totaling for 90.1% of the world's GDP (2018). Global weighted real-term price index increased by 11.4% from 2014 to 2018 (last quarter).

Country	Ref Year	GDP 2018 bnUSD	Dwellings	Other Buildings	Struct	Equipment	Biolog.	IP	Inventories
Australia	2017	1,432.2	33.5%	43.7%	77.2%	10.9%	0.4%	3.9%	7.6%
Belgium	2016	531.8	43.9%	28.6%	72.5%	16.3%	0.0%	5.0%	6.1%
Canada	2018	1,709.3	47.9%	34.6%	82.4%	7.3%	0.0%	4.3%	6.0%
France	2017	2,777.5	55.0%	24.6%	79.6%	8.0%	0.3%	5.0%	7.1%
Greece	2016	218.0	45.5%	27.8%	73.4%	17.4%	0.1%	1.6%	7.6%
Hungary	2016	155.7	24.4%	50.7%	75.1%	15.5%	0.2%	2.4%	6.8%
Israel	2017	369.7	45.5%	28.3%	73.8%	12.4%	0.3%	8.4%	5.1%
Italy	2016	2,073.9	45.6%	34.0%	79.6%	11.4%	0.1%	2.9%	6.0%
Japan	2017	4,970.9	20.2%	55.9%	76.1%	12.2%	0.0%	7.8%	3.8%
Korea	2017	1,619.4	23.4%	52.4%	75.8%	12.3%	0.2%	5.7%	5.9%
Latvia	2016	34.8	32.9%	47.6%	80.5%	12.6%	0.1%	1.2%	5.6%
Lithuania	2016	53.3	24.3%	51.4%	75.8%	13.7%	0.1%	2.4%	8.0%
Netherlands	2017	912.9	39.3%	35.2%	74.5%	14.1%	0.1%	6.7%	4.5%
New Zealand	2016	205.0	47.4%	36.9%	84.4%	11.3%	0.0%	4.3%	0.0%
Poland	2016	585.8	21.6%	46.7%	68.2%	17.3%	0.5%	2.6%	11.3%
Portugal	2016	238.0	37.9%	44.5%	82.4%	4.4%	1.1%	1.9%	10.1%
Slovak Republic	2016	106.5	21.0%	53.1%	74.1%	17.8%	2.2%	1.2%	4.7%
Slovenia	2016	54.2	30.6%	46.4%	77.0%	12.9%	0.3%	3.1%	6.7%
Sweden	2017	551.0	34.6%	33.4%	68.1%	14.1%	0.4%	7.1%	10.3%
United Kingdom	2017	2,825.2	36.5%	36.1%	72.7%	17.4%	0.2%	3.5%	6.2%
United States	2017	20,494.1	34.6%	41.6%	76.2%	12.4%	0.0%	7.1%	4.3%
Total, GDP-weigthed		**41,919**	**35.2%**	**41.2%**	**76.4%**	**12.3%**	**0.10%**	**6.1%**	**5.1%**

Figure 10: Produced assets composition (source: OECD, own analysis)

Databases for commercial properties are weaker. Qualified data are available only for eight countries, namely Brazil, Denmark, Germany, Iceland, Japan, Singapore, Switzerland, and the US. Additionally, these are more volatile and of lower quality compared to residential property data. Generally, commercial property prices tend to be more cyclical than prices of residential property. Price increases between 2014 and 2018 were evident with high regional differences, except in few countries, for example, Singapore.

In addition, these eight countries are not fully representative. They represent only 38.2% of the world's total GDP, with the US having the largest share. Furthermore, residential price growth is 20% higher in this group than in the 59-country list. Correcting the global projection for those effects, we conclude that between 2014 and 2018, the weighted global real-term property price index for commercial properties has risen by 16.5%. This value is compromised with significant accuracy risk.

The weighted mean between residential and commercial price index growth is 14.15%. This effect is not fully reflected in SNA figures. Thus, we need to conclude that the accuracy of URBAN LAND value may be compromised by a lack of appropriate revaluations in SNA statistics.

Submarine land, sea, and fish

Submarine land, thus the seabed, is not specifically owned by a private individual or government. This condition may make it difficult for World Inc. to find a counterparty for the acquisition process. Nevertheless, our approach also requires this land to be acquired and included in World Inc.'s balance sheet.

Although no trading market for submarine property exists, assigning a value to the submarine land is possible. An economic use of submarine land for fishing can be set up, similar to the relationship between pasture land and livestock. The world's fishing industry generates their catches from the use of the seas. Thus, Eq. (3) is applicable.

This approach has been applied by the World Bank in their 2018 wealth study (Lange, Wodon, and Carey 2018). Considerable effort has been spent on this matter.

However, the result is unexpected. The global rents in the fishing industry are found to be negative. Although some countries have positive returns, the majority don't have them for several reasons.

Firstly, fish stocks are overexploited. The percentages of fully fished and especially over-fished stocks have increased massively, reaching 90% in 2013 already. Consequently, the catches, have stagnated and declined.

Secondly, fish industry capacities have significantly expanded in the same years, resulting in high costs and consequently low profits.

Thirdly, the cost increases have been reduced by national fishing industry subsidies. Therefore, market exits of unprofitable fishermen have been hindered and lagged. The net results are negative rent streams. In sum, national governments spend taxpayers' subsidies to extinct fish, cease the fishing industry and deplete funds.

This situation is unattractive both from an ecological and from an economical point of view. However, to adhere to the principle of functional neutrality, we need to conclude that the fishing rent-stream and fishing values of the seas are negative.

Subsoil resources are separately accounted for, dissolved from the type of land they are found. Thus, marine subsoil resources are not included here.

Future discoveries of new sources of rents may add to the value of the seas, compensating for the overall negative fishing value. However, ecological services are in principle not included in our study. The World Bank also does not set up hypothetical value streams beyond fishing.

Thus, we conclude that as owner of the seas, World Inc. may not receive more value than it carries burden. Therefore, we follow the World Bank's conclusion to assign the value of zero to the seas.

5.3 SUBSOIL ASSETS

In Chapter 4.3, we showed that subsoil assets are not shown transparently in government balance sheets or in raw material conglomerate balance sheets. The creation of such balance sheet items therefore requires the use of many different sources and a considerable analytical effort that spans all countries and production locations.

We follow the World Bank's approach and use their results. Eq. (3) is applicable. The value of a type of subsoil asset is derived from the rents associated to it. The rents are calculated in Eq. (9) as follows:

$$R(t) = p(t)q(t)$$

Where

$R(t)$ is the rent in year t,

$p(t)$ is the calculated rent per unit, as revenue minus cost minus calculated cost of capital, and

$q(t)$ is the production in units.

In the absence of future price information, p is held constant over the lifetime of the resource.

Moreover, following the World Bank, we account separately for OIL, GAS, and COAL and the 10 most important MINERALS, namely, bauxite, copper, gold, iron ore, lead, nickel, phosphate rock, silver, tin, and zinc. For practical reasons, this analysis leverages the Pareto principle (the 80–20 rule). Therefore, less important but commercially interesting minerals need to be neglected, for example, rare earths, uranium, platinum, and titanium. World Inc. will acquire these sources at book value as reported in the balance sheet of the raw material company that exploits it. This approach leads to certain but limited underestimation of the minerals' value.

Without production, unexplored resources do not contribute a value. As discussed in Chapter 4.3, this situation results in under-representation of immature and unexplored resources.

We have modeled the 2018 values based on the World Bank's computations for 2014. The 2014 levels of rents per unit are kept constant. Asset values in 2018 are modeled from the World Bank's values in 2014 over the more recent production and lifetime statistics.

These statistics are available in good quality, and several recent statistical sources are used (International Energy Agency 2018; BP 2019; British Geological Survey 2019).

Only minor structural changes have happened since 2014. Thus far, OIL is the most commercially important subsoil asset. All SUB-SOIL ASSETS, particularly GAS and except COAL, have moderately increased their value due to production increases.

5.4   PROPERTY: CONCLUSIONS

Fig. 11 shows the asset class PROPERTY of World Inc.'s balance sheet. The world's PROPERTY in 2018 accounts for 184.01 tn USD, more than two annual world GDPs. The value is highly concentrated. That is, more than 46% of the total value is concentrated on less than 1 million km^2 urban land, and 28% are subsoil resources, which are also concentrated in a limited list of mines and sites.

Land		132.09
	Cropland	26.45
	Pasture land	16.06
	Forest	2.69
	Barren land	1.00
	Urban land	85.89
Subsoil assets		**51.91**
	Oil	30.79
	Gas	3.73
	Coal	6.85
	Minerals (10)	10.54
Property	**(tn USD 2014)**	**184.01**

Figure 11:   Property

The vast majority of the Earth's land has a comparably low economic value. Therefore, World Inc. could acquire vast areas of forests, barren land, and sea grounds at significantly low prices, with an only small amount reported in its balance sheet.

This concentration has sped up in the last years. FOREST values have deteriorated due to volume and rent stream decreases, whereas SUBSOIL ASSETS and URBAN LAND values have increased.

Plant, Equipment, Inventories

6.1 PLANT, EQUIPMENT, INVENTORIES: ACCOUNTING PRINCIPLES

The asset classes PLANT, EQUIPMENT, and INVENTORIES cannot be derived from company balance sheets or commercial accounting results. We rely on the SNA data, which are consolidated and integrated by global data integrators such as World Bank, IMF, OECD, and PWT. They make the database reliable, detailed, and significant. However, we have to deal with severe accuracy issues that require further sources and methodological extensions.

The SNA definitions of assets, particularly produced assets, generally do not match the commercial definitions of the IFRS.

Relatively best is the situation with buildings. Categorized as PLANT, they mark a relatively well-defined asset category. We can identify this IFRS term well with the SNA term "structures". Therefore, World Inc.'s asset type PLANT includes all buildings for residential, commercial, and civil engineering use.

Equipment is a subtype of Fixed Capital; Inventories belong to Working Capital; and durable consumption goods are not considered an asset by the SNA. Theoretically and practically, equipment, inventories, and durable consumer goods are not clearly separated with regard to SNA statistics due to several reasons.

The SNA's definition of an asset is relatively narrow compared with that of commercial accounting practice. As defined in the SNA:

> "Assets are entities that must be owned by some unit, or units, and from which economic benefits are derived by their owner(s) by holding or using them over a period of time." (United Nations et al. 2011, 1.46, p. 65)

All constituting elements of this definition create issues in statistical practice. Not in all cases owning units can be assigned to (potential) assets, for instance, in the case of subsoil resources, which typically have no owner in accounting terms.

The requirement of derived economic benefits, that is, value streams, is also a challenge as SNA's value stream view has an arbitrary component. Although these value streams are set up by the SNA for private buildings, the SNA prohibits such approach for equipment.

> "Machinery and equipment cover transport equipment, machinery for information, communication and telecommunications (ICT) equipment, and other machinery and equipment." (United Nations et al. 2011, 10.82, p. 204).

These chattels are distributed to companies, private households, and governmental institutions. Neither governments nor private households account for value streams obtained from these items. Thus, a significant portion of equipment may be accounted for in different categories.

Also, the "use over a period" poses practical issues. For example, inventories are assets with expected turnaround within a year.

Considering that the SNA employs the calendar year as the accounting year, short-term accounting faces certain challenges.

> "The estimation of nominal holding gains on inventories may be difficult because of lack of data on transactions or other volume changes in inventories…. transactions in inventories of work-in-progress and finished goods may not be adequately recorded because they are internal transactions." (United Nations et al. 2011, 12.97, p. 251).

Furthermore, many inventories are owned by private households and governments; they are purchased for consumption purposes and therefore no assets. Consequentially, several countries do not report INVENTORIES for the SNA or explicitly report the value at zero. Reporting for EQUIPMENT is better but still limited to a minor part of the international community.

Therefore, leveraging SNA statistics for worldwide estimation of EQUIPMENT and INVENTORIES generates a risk of underestimation. Only equipment and inventories associated with (commercial) value streams are adequately reported. The SNA focuses on assets owned by commercial businesses. Hence, in our study, we will refer to the SNA-denominated value for equipment and inventories as COMMERCIAL EQUIPMENT and COMMERCIAL INVENTORIES, respectively.

6.2 PLANT

The IFRS asset class PLANT includes all buildings World Inc. acquires. Estimating the total asset value has certain issues.

Firstly, two issues discussed in Chapter 4.2 are present here. PLANT value is derived from the total capital stock, which is modeled following the PIM method. The higher the longevity of an asset is, and the longer the service life, the less accurate the PIM method proves to be. On average, buildings have the longest service lives among all fixed assets. Thus, the accuracy of their value estimation is compromised most.

Secondly, this service life is not well-standardized globally. Global institutions operating the SNA have never pressed the national statistic agencies to introduce globally uniform building service lives, because buildings are not a homogeneous category. For instance, tropical buildings may be made of bamboo, wood, and other perishable materials and thus have shorter service lives compared with concrete buildings in some countries. In these countries, the culture requests children to reuse the house of their parents, and in such countries, every generation builds new houses. These differences are rightfully cited when following a decentralized valuation approach. If the same asset type in different countries shows significantly different service life, then this difference may be due to reasonable circumstances.

However, these differences are mostly less well founded. Although statistical agencies appropriately monitor the asset production, asset disposal is not given much consideration. Therefore, arbitrary service lives dominate national statistics. Tax laws are a major source of national service life parameters as they are the basis of determining the depreciable life of buildings, equipment, and other assets. Tax laws reflect less accurately real service lives. Instead, they incentivize the production of certain assets with accelerated depreciation. These laws are implemented in companies' commercial accounting, resulting in shorter statistical service lives compared with actual service lives. Thus, many assets still produce value despite being written off by the company.

In a detailed study the Statistical agency of the Netherlands found that many assets have surprisingly long real service lives (Meinen, Verbiest, and Wolf 1998). For example, civil engineering buildings (bridges, canals, tunnels, and infrastructure) have service lives of more than 100 years. In addition, dwellings in some countries are used longer than a century, too. This finding leads to underestimation of buildings' asset value over their actual service life.

This effect becomes apparent when considering transfer prices of antique buildings, such the Pyramids of Giza and the Acropolis, to World Inc. This means that the SNA book value of these buildings is either zero or extremely low, only taking into account the maintenance effort of recent years, not for the actual remaining service life of the building. World Inc. will be positively surprised by how it can acquire these famous sites of world cultural heritage at extremely low prices based on their SNA book value.

This situation suggests the last major issue, that is, SNA asset accounting is "at cost," thus accruing the output of building industry. Despite the official requirement of revaluation (see Chapter 4.2), market transfer price changes for buildings are not completely and reliably reflected in the SNA data, as already discussed in Chapter 5.2 (urban land). Thus, we estimate the value of the asset class PLANT using Eq. (10) as follows:

$$P_i = p \cdot s_i$$

Where

P_i is the value of building type i,

p is the value of total produced assets, and

s_i is the proportion of the building type i in the total produced assets.

s_i is derived from detailed produced asset composition data of 21 OECD countries (Fig. 10).

Data accuracy issues of fixed assets become evident and quantifiable when we examine data sources. Different global data integrators (the World Bank, IMF, and PWT) report different fixed asset values, despite relying on the SNA. They use different approaches in their secondary data processing to counter the issues mentioned.

PWT 9.1 (Feenstra, Inklaar, and Timmer 2015) provides an interesting data source for globally comparable fixed assets that addresses specific issues within the databases.

For example, the heterogeneous service lives of fixed assets are standardized across all countries. Six classes of investments are differentiated, each of which is assigned a fixed service life across the globe (e.g., 50 years for buildings). The question of asset price developments is reflected and integrated, which means that a large vector of prices is held constant across countries and years. This approach allows annual country-level comparison within certain confidence intervals. Output comparability is given emphasis (comparison of value flows), making PWT highly interesting for our purpose. The quality is homogeneous and high. Nearly all countries are covered relatively timely, so that data are broader and quicker than the ones of World Bank or IMF.

These essential advantages are offset by two disadvantages.

Holding the price vector constant requires the need to adopt a PPP model for international value comparisons. This approach diverts from the principle of buying at market prices (see Chapter 3.3), which includes purchase of foreign currencies at current exchange rates. World Inc. accounts in USD and therefore will find it relatively expensive to acquire assets in foreign countries based on PPP evaluations (PPP model effect). Local currencies can be acquired at lower prices on average.

Secondly, PWT data are not directly comparable with those from other sources, especially the World Bank and IMF, because country information has been modified at the base already (own data completion rules, own PIM models).

For the purposes of this study, we consider PWT 9.1 as superior reliable data source compared with the World Bank and IMF. To comply with the principles of this study, we have corrected country-level PWT data with the price level of GDP measured in 2014 USD/local PPP. This correction compensates PWT's PPP model effect and improves data compliance with market price acquisition principle. We have decided to use PPP-corrected PWT 9.1 as the most focused and timely data source for the quantification of World Inc.'s produced assets. Nevertheless, PWT still entails certain inaccuracy drivers mentioned above including underestimation of long-term assets and the weaknesses of PIM and CFA.

By leveraging Eq. (10), we find the value of the world DWELLINGS and all OTHER BUILDINGS in 2018 as 119.84 tn USD and 140.43 tn USD, respectively. Thus, World Inc.'s asset category PLANT accounts for 260.27 tn USD in total.

6.3   EQUIPMENT

Commercial Equipment

We derive COMMERCIAL EQUIPMENT from PPP-corrected PWT 9.1 by projecting OECD's composition of produced capital (Fig. 10). In 2018, World Inc. reports 41.98 tn USD of COMMERCIAL EQUIPMENT.

Military Equipment

Further equipment asset class exists other than COMMERCIAL EQUIPMENT. Since 2008, the SNA includes "Weapon Systems" in their asset accounting:

> "Expenditures on military equipment, including large military weapons systems, are treated as fixed capital formation." (United Nations et al. 2011, 6.232, p 180).

> "Weapon systems include vehicles and other equipment such as warships, submarines, military aircraft, tanks, missile carriers and launchers, etc." (United Nations et al. 2011, 10.87, p 204).

The SNA does not refer to the question of which economic value stream is created by warships and tanks in detail and how this stipulation meets the general criteria of SNA's asset definition. However, the stipulation correctly reflects the facts that MILITARY EQUIPMENT is durable, has a market price, and needs to be acquired by World Inc.

Unfortunately, the international community has not implemented SNA 2008 in this case. No major military power has reported on MILITARY EQUIPMENT at present. Because many countries treat these figures as matter of national security, they are kept confidential.

This secretive stance of military powers compromises not only SNA reporting but also reporting of other data aggregators. Therefore, estimation of MILITARY EQUIPMENT value entails high accuracy risk, which is also true for our estimation. Alternatively, the assumption that World Inc. could acquire all MILITARY EQUIPMENT of the world's military powers for free is not a viable approach.

Hence, we rely on our own analysis due to insufficient integrative studies. Fortunately, the Stockholm International Peace Research Institute (SIPRI) provides extensive data about global military expenditures, which are well accepted in the international community. To estimate the world's MILITARY EQUIPMENT, we leverage SIPRI data in setting up a PIM model (SIPRI 2018, 2019b, 2019a).

SIPRI also criticizes the lack of transparency in reporting:

> "Military expenditure transparency at the international level remains a concern, specifically in the context of the United Nations Report on Military Expenditures. By July 31 2017… no submission had been received from any state in Africa or the Middle East or from four of the five largest military spenders in the world…Continued low participation in, and the lack of comprehensiveness of, the UN reporting mechanism puts into question its future viability." (SIPRI 2018, p. 7)

According to SIPRI, the world's total military expenditure in 2018 is 1,899 bn USD (2014). However, the investment share of this amount into weapon systems is not directly reported due to the decentralized nature of the sources utilized. Thus, a more indirect approach needs to be employed. SIPRI tracks the production of the world's top 100 arms-producing companies. In 2017, the total arms revenue of these top 100 companies is 415.9 bn USD (2014).

Since only the top 100 are captured, underestimation risks of the total global arms production arise. By definition, small companies are excluded from the list. Some major companies are also not captured because some producers do not disclose their figures.

SIPRI explicitly mentions Chinese producers, which could not be completely included in their statistics.

However, other data point in the opposite direction, i.e., overestimation. Not all produced weapons are purchased by military. Some end in private households and are accounted for under CONSUMER DURABLES. Some other products of the arms industry are not durable, for example, ammunition and other disposables.

The major product groups of MILITARY EQUIPMENT, namely, warships, military aircraft, armored vehicles, and artillery, require large and specialized companies for production. Therefore, it is reasonable to assume that the overwhelming part of their value is produced by the companies included in SIPRI's list. A brief cross-checking underpins further the viability of the approach. The total arms revenues of SIPRI's top 100 companies equal 21.9% of the world's military spending. According to the UN, in 2017, the overall gross capital formation quota of the world's GDP was 25.7%. It is reasonable to expect a military investment rate at the same level.

Therefore, we decided to accept SIPRI's top 100 arms production figure as the best available estimation for total gross investment into military equipment. These data exist since 2002.

To set up a PIM model, we need to make assumptions on military equipment service lives. However, systematic data aggregations are not available. Furthermore, military equipment types have different service lives, which vary widely across organizations. Belligerent nations tend to replace their equipment faster than peaceful countries, which complicates global data integration. If not used, some equipment can have unusually long service lives. Anecdotal evidences exist for service lives of more than 50 years, such as for aircraft carriers, strategic bombers, and nuclear bombs.

Different coherent data points are used for service lives. For instance, the average service life of 52 historic aircraft carriers has been 29 years. In addition, planes are considered to have 25 years of service life. Many armored vehicles, having been developed in the 1980s, remain in service for more than 20 years. Infantry weapons are replaced more frequently. Generally, smaller weaponry tends to have shorter service lives. However, due to insufficient data, establishing a differentiated service life model is not viable.

Thus, we have to estimate the mean service life of MILITARY EQUIPMENT to 25 years. In accordance with SIPRI general observations, our PIM model shows an increase in MILITARY EQUIPMENT in recent years, totaling to 8.74 tn USD (2014) in 2018.

6.4   INVENTORIES

Commercial Inventories

Similar to PLANT and EQUIPMENT, we derive COMMERCIAL INVENTORIES from PPP-corrected PWT 9.1 by projecting OECD produced capital composition (Fig. 10). Thus, World Inc. reports 17.54 tn USD of COMMERCIAL INVENTORIES in 2018.

Consumer Durables

Consumers own the majority of durable goods, which we collectively refer to as CONSUMER DURABLES. Examples of consumer durable goods include automobiles, books, household goods (home appliances, consumer electronics, furniture, tools, etc.), sports equipment, jewelry, medical equipment, and firearms. Although many of these chattels have active markets, these markets are fragmented, and globally integrated statistics are scarce. Due to the lack of private balance sheets, identifying the exact owners of these assets can be difficult. For example, within families, ownership matters are frequently debated (Doss, Kieran, and Kilic 2017).

Cars form a major part of consumer durables. In 2018, approximately 1.44 billion cars were registered globally, representing a substantial financial value. Many of these cars are owned by leasing companies and fleet management firms that account for them. However, the majority of these assets are owned by private households. Although World Inc. acquires company-owned cars during the acquisition of companies, private cars need to be acquired from each household separately. The same process applies to all other consumer durables.

Strict application of the IFRS rules bottom-up could lead to accounting of durable goods in different asset types, depending on the detailed purpose of each durable item. For example, some cars could be reported either as EQUIPMENT or INVENTORIES. Given this weak data that render accurate assignment of separate assets generally impossible, we prefer to account for the entire CONSUMER DURABLES in one asset type in World Inc.'s balance sheet.

It can be argued to account for consumer durables as EQUIPMENT considering that they are used for several years and commercial uses for certain consumer durables are possible (e.g., cars, boats, art, and antiquities). However, we opted to account for consumer durables as INVENTORIES. Commercial fleet management companies tend to report rental cars as INVENTORIES rather than EQUIPMENT. The main purpose of household durables is consumption over time. Thus, quantifiable rent streams are mostly absent and not accounted for in the SNA and other economical aggregations.

To estimate the global value of consumer durables, we rely on statistics from OECD. However, OECD has reported the structure of household non-financial assets only until 2014. Within this limited dataset, we have found that the structure of private non-financial assets is relatively stable over time and across countries. By far, the largest part in private non-financial assets comprises DWELLINGS, followed by CONSUMER DURABLES. OTHER BUILDINGS and EQUIPMENT mark only small portions, which are already accounted for in the respective asset types. In average, we found that CONSUMER DURABLES account for 24.5% of DWELLINGS. As a structural, intrinsic parameter, it slowly changes in time. Therefore, it forms the basis of our global projection.

We estimate the total value of the world's CONSUMER DURABLES to 29.36 tn USD in 2018.

7

Intangible Assets

7.1 INTANGIBLE ASSETS: DEFINITIONS AND ACCOUNTING PRINCIPLES

An intangible asset is an asset that lacks physical substance. However, not all assets that lack physical substance belong to the asset class INTANGIBLE ASSETS. IFRS (and other accounting frameworks) exclude all financial assets from this definition.

> "An intangible asset is an identifiable non-monetary asset without physical substance." (IFRS 2019).

Therefore, asset types such as accounts receivables are not summarized under INTANGIBLE ASSETS, though they evidently lack physical substance.

Based on the concept of monovalent assets previously discussed, we can define INTANGIBLE ASSETS, for the purposes of this study, as monovalent assets without physical substance.

Accordingly, INTANGIBLE ASSETS are defined negatively as a remainder. A common finite positive definition of intangible assets has not been established. Several differentiated asset types fulfill the definition. In a certain sense, the asset class is open for future revisions.

Fig. 12 gives an overview about frequently used intangible asset categories. These assets are disclosed in companies' balance sheets and are acquired by World Inc. Thus, the balance sheet of World Inc. needs to reflect the total of all companies' balance sheets in each category.

Asset category	Example	Asset type
Marketing-related	Trademark	Brand value
	Newspaper mastheads	
	Internet domain names	
Customer-related	Customer relationships	
	Order backlog	
	Customer lists	
Artistic-related	Literary works	Intellectual property
	Musical works	
	Pictures	
Technology-based	Patents	
	Software	
	Trade secrets	
Contract-based	Licensing agreements	Licenses
	Broadcast rights	
	Use rights	
Company value	Goodwill	Goodwill

Figure 12:   Intangible assets

Due to heterogeneity of these assets, the quality of available data determines the possible resolution. Thus, we have decided to differentiate four types of INTANGIBLE ASSETS, namely, BRAND VALUE, INTELLECTUAL PROPERTY, LICENSES, and GOODWILL as shown in Fig. 12.

7.2 DATA SOURCES

Reporting of intangible assets in the SNA (United Nations et al. 2011) is rudimentary. No Intangible Asset type, as shown in Fig. 12, is reported in SNA, except for IP. Therefore, SNA and SNA-reliant sources are not providing quality data. According to the SNA valuation, all companies can be acquired at their tangible book value by World Inc., which clearly does not reflect the real value.

Second-tier sources are also scarce. OECD frequently leads economic data collection and provision, but does not systematically provide intangible asset data for their member states. Even the root data provision of companies about their intangible assets is seen critically by OECD. In a 2012 review, OECD states that accounting quality of intangible assets remains inconsistent. Many companies do not report intangible assets or focus only on specific assets that are strategically important. According to this report, a systematic overview of all company intangible assets is the exception. Furthermore, national recommendations are more anecdotal, and international comparability is insufficient. Therefore,

> "For all of the reasons enumerated above, reporting on intangibles remains controversial and relatively slow to develop." (Amico 2012, p. 19).

This constraint makes us strongly reliant on few second-tier and mostly third-tier sources, which exist in the financial markets that focus on public companies and specific banking establishments. Furthermore, heterogeneous sources are available for non-listed private companies and SOEs. For these reasons, INTANGIBLE ASSETS carry a particularly high accuracy risk in this study.

7.3 GOODWILL: VALUE OF ACQUIRED COMPANIES

World Inc. acquires all companies at market prices. In general terms, the market price will be typically higher than the book value. After every company acquisition, World Inc. consolidates the company's assets as disclosed in the company's balance sheet, consisting of (1) tangible assets, and (2) disclosed INTANGIBLE ASSETS. Moreover,

World Inc. will book a third category of (3) previously undisclosed INTANGIBLE ASSETS, which will cover the difference of the acquisition price and the total disclosed book value. Primarily, this will be accounted for as GOODWILL by World Inc.

Listed companies

For listed companies, who disclose their balance sheet, the data situation has improved during the last years, due to early second-tier studies. Of particular importance are the annual GIFT studies of Brand Finance. The objective of these studies (GIFT: Global Intangible Finance Tracker) is the creation of an overview of the Intangible Assets of global listed companies. Originally, accounting and reporting gaps were in the foreground.

> "At Brand Finance, we started to study the value of companies' intangible assets in 2001 principally to show the glaring inaccuracies of financial statements globally due to the underreporting of intangible asset values." (Haigh et al. 2018, p 12).

We follow the methodology and results of the 2018 study. Including possibly all listed companies in banking centers around the world, Brand Value finds a total market capitalization of 109.2 tn USD for 2018. 65.6 tn USD of those are disclosed book value, 43.7 tn USD are non-disclosed. That is, the average price-to-book ratio (P/B) globally has been found as 1.66. Of the 65.6 tn USD book value, 13.6 tn USD are disclosed INTANGIBLE ASSETS. Of those, 5.6 tn USD are detailed INTANGIBLE ASSETS (BRAND VALUE and LICENSES), whereas 8.0 tn USD are undifferentiated GOODWILL from previous acquisitions.

Therefore, after the acquisition of these listed companies, World Inc. will book 5.6 tn USD BRAND VALUE and LICENSES and 51.7 tn USD GOODWILL. (The disclosed tangible assets have already been included in the previous chapters). It is well understood that this GOODWILL can contain further components of specific INTANGIBLE ASSETS (BRAND VALUE, LICENSES, INTELLECTUAL PROPERTY).

GOODWILL finally is a remainder asset type within the remainder asset class INTANGIBLE ASSETS.

Brand Value, like OECD and other authors, remarks a clear tendency to underreport on INTANGIBLE ASSETS; therefore, 5.6 tn USD as non-goodwill intangibles is probably an underestimation. The total, however, has reasonably good accuracy, since the market prices of stock-listed companies are transparent and well-documented.

Non-listed private companies

Whereas World Inc.'s acquisition of listed companies can be well constructed, supported by financial data and some second-tier studies, this looks more complicated with other companies. Statistics for companies directly complementary to listed companies do not exist; companies are too heterogeneous in size, ownership, and regulation. Additionally, the political interest to monitor them is more limited.

The relative best is the situation for non-listed private companies, which have private holders and can be traded. However, literature to estimate values of non-listed private companies remains limited. A rare example is Anderson (Anderson 2009), who examines the non-listed private business sector in the US and concludes the value of this sector to exceed the value of listed companies. On a global scale, a study conducted in 2016 calculated the value of private companies (Gadzinski, Schuller, and Vacchino 2016). In a relatively simple approximation model, the authors concluded that the total value of non-listed private businesses exceeds listed companies' value by around 50%.

Fortunately, however, the vast majority of private non-listed companies are known as SMEs (Small and Medium-Sized Enterprises). For SMEs, a certain reporting and monitoring has evolved in the last years, which allows us to address this important segment (Eurostat 2018). We use SMEs, therefore, as a proxy of non-listed private companies in accordance with literature.

We need to be aware, however, that this approach still comes with a significant inaccuracy risk for the following reasons:

- Not all listed companies are large companies beyond 250 employees, measured in full-time equivalents (FTEs). Some listed companies can be small in employment, yet valuable, for example, digital enterprises or patent boxes.
- Not all large companies are listed. Large corporations exist in family ownership or as private companies. Many of those have values beyond 1 bn USD ("unicorns"). This issue causes a risk of underestimation.
- Some large companies are active mainly in country A, but listed at a foreign stock exchange in country B. This can distort the country assignment of value creation, and thus, the valuation.
- Many large listed corporations own small SMEs in foreign countries, for instance, as sales subsidiaries. From the perspective of the corporation, these subsidiaries are consolidated in the parent company's balance sheet. In the host country's view, these are SMEs contributing to the country's GDP. This causes a risk of double counting, and therefore, overestimation.

Nevertheless, this approach seems to be the only viable one. With more detailed data being made available in recent years, we can provide a more detailed estimation than Gadzinski et al., based on country-by-country modeling.

Small and Medium-Sized Enterprises (SMEs)

Small and medium-sized enterprises have caught political attention during the last few years. The first political body to invest significantly in science and statistical effort has been the European Union. The tenth European Commission's annual report on European SMEs (Muller et al. 2018) is comprehensive and rich in data. The work of the EU has trickled down to OECD in recent years, and other major countries have also intensified their work on SMEs.

According to the EU's definition (European Union 2003), companies up to 250 FTEs are called SMEs (within certain limits of balance sheet size and turnover). Whereas other countries partly have different limits, the EU's definition has proven to be influential; the 250 FTE cutoff is used by a majority of countries today.

Globally, and in a vast majority of countries, SMEs produce more than 50% of GDP. Their share of employment is frequently even greater. The reason for this is the sheer number of enterprises. The exact numbers of companies are available only for few legislations. The European Union in 2018 counts 24,483,496 SMEs, but only 46,547 large enterprises (>250 FTE) (Muller et al. 2018, p15). Large numbers are also counted in India, China, and the US. Global total numbers are estimated to be between 200 and 300 million SMEs.

One would assume that listed companies would structurally outperform SMEs, thus resulting in higher valuations than the latter: management is paid better, transparency is higher, and pressure of financial markets pushes for efficiency. These and other arguments may support the assumption of better performance, and thus valuations, of listed companies.

Science and statistics, however, do not support this assumption. The European Union finds that, in the ten years after the financial crisis (2008-2018), SMEs have increased their share of economy and performed slightly better than the EU's large corporations (Muller et al. 2018). Many comparative examinations on family businesses conclude their performance to be superior to that of listed companies. Small caps in many places tend to outperform large caps in long-term studies. Creation of IP tends to be higher in mid-size companies than in large caps.

Data situation, therefore, complies well with the assumption that the valuation parameters of listed companies can be projected to non-listed companies without introducing a major inaccuracy risk. Common valuation parameters are P/E (price/earnings ratio: Price of a company, as a multiple of its annual earnings), and P/B (price/book ratio: Price of a company, as a multiple of its book value). We assume, therefore, the same multiples for P/E and P/B in the listed and the non-listed segments of private businesses.

These multiples, however, differ widely by country and with industry mix. We therefore set up a global analysis by country to draw a differentiated picture of each country's contribution to listed and non-listed enterprise value.

Various sources of the financial services industry provide market capitalization studies by country; we use StarCapital's analysis (StarCapital AG 2019). Since stock prices show high fluctuations, and countries perform differently, the relative weights of countries are volatile.

We use value-added as the best measure of SME output. This metric can be derived from SNA data and is available through different sources. EU countries are covered by the EU (Muller et al. 2018) and some more OECD countries are reported by OECD (OECD 2017a). For many other countries, specific monographies have been made available in recent years: Japan (National Association of Small and Medium Enterprise Promotion Organizations 2018), India (Arya 2017), Canada (Innovation, Science and Economic Development Canada 2019), Korea (Ministry of SMEs and Startups 2019), Indonesia (Burger et al. 2015), Malaysia (Department of Statistics Malaysia 2019), Norway (Alba 2014), Singapore (Singapore Department of Statistics 2018). Since the SME share of value-added in a national economy is an intrinsic (structural) parameter, it changes slowly. Therefore, we have also accepted older data (back to 2014) to be projected into 2018.

Several important countries, however, are not well-documented: Russia had a strongly concentrated industry during socialism. Today, the share of SMEs in the total economy remains limited and clearly smaller than in average OECD countries. Based on several sources, particularly OECD (OECD 2015), we estimate that the share of SMEs of Russian value-added is 25% in 2018. The important segment of state-owned companies, which is also not well documented, could further distort the estimates for Russia.

China has a huge SME sector as reported in the Chinese Statistics yearbook. Definitions and limits, however, are different from the EU/OECD, which jeopardizes the comparability. Additionally, the large segment of state-owned enterprises and the fact that Chinese-listed companies are partly listed in Hong Kong, partly in China, but partly also in the US and in other countries, may also distort the figures.

The US, finally, does not provide statistical SME value-added data on a national level. The agency responsible for SMEs - the US Small Business Administration -uses specific definitions not compliant with EU and OECD standards, and does not release annual reports. Data indicate, however, that the relative importance of SMEs is somewhat smaller than in other developed countries. The most comprehensive, but older, study (Bookman and et al. 2010) analyzes the value contribution in detail and concludes the SME share of value-added to be 43.9%. Since the relative importance of the US is so high, this relative uncertainty introduces a specific inaccuracy risk.

Figures are available for countries representing 95.3% of market capitalization. For the remaining countries (Rest of World) we assume OECD mean SME value-added share. The intangible part of this is projected according to the GIFT study (Haigh et al. 2018). In contrast to listed companies, non-listed private companies do not disclose defined non-goodwill INTANGIBLE ASSETS like BRAND VALUE, LICENSES, or IP. Their total book value therefore corresponds to the tangible book value of listed companies, which we reflect in the valuation.

The result is shown in Fig. 13. We find that driven by the acquisition of the world's SMEs World Inc. will need to book additional 72.7 tn USD INTANGIBLE ASSETS. Since no intangible assets have been disclosed in the acquired companies' balance sheets, we cannot say which part of this may be brand or license value. We book the total as GOODWILL, after correction for INTELLECTUAL PROPERTY (see 7.5).

State-owned Enterprises (SOEs)

A further, frequently-neglected group of companies is the group of state-owned enterprises (SOEs). These are enterprises in full or majority ownership of central or regional governments. In the absence of balance sheets, and with different targets compared to commercial companies, and thus, with different financial valuation parameters, this group has proven most difficult to capture.

Fortunately, however, the generally thorny data situation has improved recently.

In their 2015 study (Price Waterhouse Coopers 2015), PWC analyzed this sector and its global development in recent years. SOEs have been existing since decades, particularly in emerging and transitional economies, as well as in many European countries. PWC has found that (2014) 23% of the Fortune 500 companies have been SOEs, with accumulated revenues of more than 8 tn USD. In 2005, only 9% of Fortune 500 companies had been SOEs. The main driver behind this development is the growth of China, which has an enormous SOE sector larger than all other SOEs of the world combined.

The very detailed OECD study (OECD 2017b) about SOEs in 40 OECD countries and beyond, including China, analyzes thousands of SOEs bottom-up. 2,467 enterprises with over 9.2 M employees operate in 39 countries, excluding China. In China alone, 159,198 SOEs with 40.1 M employees have been analyzed. For our study, only non-listed companies are included to avoid double counting. Values for SOEs have been directly estimated by OECD (OECD 2017b). We use this analysis as direct source.

SOEs are, however, not directly comparable to listed companies when it comes to valuation ratios. Price-to-book ratios of SOEs are reasonable to be lower than in listed companies for several reasons.

Country	Weight	Private VA%	Listed value	Listed Goodwill	SME value	SME Intangible	SOE value	SOE Intangible
Australia	2.0%	54.4%	2,185.4	872.5	2,628.5	1,376.9	13.6	3.4
Austria	0.2%	61.8%	218.5	87.3	361.4	189.3	4.9	1.2
Belgium	0.6%	62.4%	655.6	261.8	1,088.1	569.9	0.0	0.0
Brazil	1.5%	50.2%	1,639.1	654.4	1,800.0	942.9	145.0	36.0
Canada	3.0%	50.2%	3,278.1	1,308.8	3,335.0	1,746.9	30.3	7.5
China	1.7%	64.3%	1,857.6	741.7	25,315.7	13,260.6	12,197.9	638.9
Czech Rep	0.0%	54.7%	43.7	17.5	52.8	27.6	0.0	0.0
Denmark	0.6%	60.0%	655.6	261.8	1,003.6	525.7	13.5	3.3
Finland	0.4%	60.9%	437.1	174.5	743.6	389.5	40.3	10.0
France	4.0%	55.2%	4,370.8	1,745.1	5,480.2	2,870.6	76.9	19.1
Germany	3.0%	54.0%	3,278.1	1,308.8	3,932.7	2,060.0	72.0	17.9
Greece	0.1%	63.6%	109.3	43.6	336.6	176.3	83.4	20.7
Hong Kong	4.1%	64.3%	4,480.1	1,788.7	8,069.1	4,226.7	0.0	0.0
Hungary	0.0%	53.7%	43.7	17.5	61.2	32.1	9.1	2.3
India	2.7%	45.0%	2,950.3	1,177.9	2,690.8	1,409.5	338.5	100.5
Indonesia	0.6%	57.0%	655.6	261.8	869.1	455.2	0.0	0.0
Ireland	0.1%	41.7%	109.3	43.6	85.5	44.8	10.2	2.5
Israel	0.2%	62.7%	218.5	87.3	367.7	192.6	0.0	0.0
Italy	1.0%	67.1%	1,092.7	436.3	2,651.8	1,389.0	207.5	51.5
Japan	8.4%	54.4%	9,178.7	3,664.6	11,048.3	5,787.2	82.4	20.4
Korea	1.4%	51.2%	1,529.8	610.8	1,833.5	960.4	217.8	54.0
Malaysia	0.5%	38.3%	546.4	218.1	339.1	177.6	0.0	0.0
Mexico	0.5%	38.5%	546.4	218.1	354.9	185.9	21.2	5.3
Netherlands	1.1%	61.8%	1,202.0	479.9	2,078.7	1,088.8	82.9	20.6
Norway	0.4%	71.4%	437.1	174.5	1,360.4	712.6	107.9	26.8
Philippines	0.4%	35.7%	437.1	174.5	242.7	127.1	0.0	0.0
Poland	0.2%	51.4%	218.5	87.3	247.8	129.8	15.7	3.9
Portugal	0.1%	68.4%	109.3	43.6	236.5	123.9	0.0	0.0
Russia	1.0%	25.0%	1,092.7	436.3	364.2	190.8	0.0	0.0
Singapore	0.8%	49.0%	874.2	349.0	839.9	439.9	0.0	0.0
Spain	1.1%	62.2%	1,202.0	479.9	2,038.3	1,067.7	36.7	9.1
Sweden	0.9%	59.7%	983.4	392.6	1,511.8	791.9	37.1	9.2
Switzerland	2.6%	57.9%	2,841.0	1,134.3	3,961.5	2,075.1	44.7	11.1
Turkey	0.2%	53.9%	218.5	87.3	328.4	172.0	62.5	15.5
United Kingdom	4.6%	51.1%	5,026.4	2,006.8	5,372.4	2,814.1	114.6	28.4
United States	45.2%	43.9%	49,390.0	19,719.2	38,649.2	20,244.8	0.0	0.0
Rest Of World	4.7%	56.8%	5,135.7	2,050.5	7,167.4	3,754.4	315.6	78.3
World (bn USD)	100.0%	56.0%	109,248.1	43,617.9	138,848.7	72,730.3	14,382.4	1,197.4

Figure 13: Company values: Listed companies, SMEs, SOEs

Firstly, SOEs are concentrated in infrastructural industries, transportation, energy, and utilities. These industries are relatively capital intensive and have lower P/B ratios than average listed companies generally.

Secondly, the objectives of SOEs differ from sheer profit maximation. Regional development, avoidance of monopolies, economic growth, and social welfare are frequent objectives mixing with economic objectives. Therefore, lower profitability compared with listed companies can be expected.

Evidence supports this expectation. P/B ratios of SOEs can be studied with listed companies, which are completely or majorly in the ownership of states. We have used these as benchmarks for non-listed SOEs as well. Due to its importance, we have derived a specific SOE P/B ratio for China based on the OECD dataset. We have found it to be only 1.055. For India, with the second largest SOE sector worldwide, we could derive a P/B of 1.42. For the Rest of the World, we use a P/B of 1.33. These values are lower than the ones of listed companies, yet indicate a considerable intangible value of SOEs.

Fig. 13 indicates that non-listed SOEs worldwide represent an estimated trade value of 14.4 tn USD. 1.20 tn USD need to be booked by World Inc. as INTANGIBLE ASSETS after the acquisition of all these companies. We book the total as GOODWILL, after correction for INTELLECTUAL PROPERTY (see 7.5).

7.4   INTANGIBLE GOVERNMENTAL ASSETS

World Inc. also acquires all governments, including their authorities, agencies, and assets. We need to examine whether some of these entities have intangible assets that have not been previously recognized.

Unfortunately, data basis as well as theoretical foundations are weak. Only a very slim minority of governments creates their own balance sheets, and those are not appropriately standardized to allow the integration of proper global views.

Within SNA, governmental assets are monitored as a share of produced assets. This allows governmental produced assets to be estimated as a share of the total produced assets, which some major data aggregators do (IMF 2017, 2019). These assets are included in Chapter 6 already, consequentially. Since government expenditure is considered consumption, no values for authorities are assumed beyond the fixed asset value. Therefore, neither estimations for intangible assets nor estimations of market values for public agencies can be derived from these SNA-based sources.

Furthermore, a market or price finding mechanism for public authorities is widely missing and controversially discussed in literature.

We have reasons to believe that public agencies have relatively small amounts of intangible capital, if any. State-owned enterprises already have a relatively small share of intangible capital compared with private businesses. We have seen that this is driven by a blend of commercial and non-commercial objectives. Public authorities and agencies now have no commercially-focused objectives at all. Thus, public services do not provide a value stream in the sense of commercial accounting. Furthermore, the transactional nature of these services does not favor activities leading to intangible assets (Fig. 12): marketing and consumer-related activities, artistic-related and contract-based activities, and mergers and acquisitions. These kinds of activities are untypical for public agencies.

There may be an exception, however. Particularly in security services - armed forces, intelligence community, police, etc. - public agencies have to be competitive, and thus, innovative, which leads to technology-based activities and consecutive creation of IP. For example, the NSA may have significant intellectual property that is also useful to a commercial acquirer such as World Inc. Due to national security considerations, however, relevant data are not available to derive a substantial direct estimation.

Worldwide listed companies disclose only 5.60 tn USD as discrete non-goodwill INTANGIBLE ASSETS. Given the smaller size of the governmental sector (ex SOEs), the small P/B ratios of SOEs compared to listed companies, and the different nature of public agencies compared to private companies, we feel entitled to neglect the contribution of public agencies to the INTANGIBLE ASSETS of World Inc. World Inc. thus acquires all public agencies, including agencies like NSA, for their tangible book value only; any potential intangible assets are acquired for free. Obviously, this creates a certain risk of underestimation of World Inc.'s INTANGIBLE ASSETS, particularly its INTELLECTUAL PROPERTY.

7.5 INTELLECTUAL PROPERTY

INTELLECTUAL PROPERTY is the only asset type of INTANGIBLE ASSETS, which is reported upon in the SNA (since 2008). SNA assumes INTELLECTUAL PROPERTY to be a part of Fixed Capital. The SNA model, in brief, is the following:

- The performance of Research and Development (R&D) is gross fixed capital formation of intellectual property products (IPPs).
- The result of the R&D is an original asset.

An advantage of this concept is its relatively easy applicability. Just by monitoring the R&D costs of a country its intellectual property creation can be calculated. Many countries report IP as a fraction of produced capital (Fig. 10), although the implementation of SNA 2008 is not yet fully finalized.

The SNA concept, however, is insular. Firstly, it is in conflict with commercial accounting. In commercial accounting, not all R&D activities create assets. Furthermore, non-R&D activities can lead to IP creation, namely, artist activities, and technological and other processes (Fig. 12).

Additionally, the SNA model creates specific accuracy issues since its definitions are in conflict with some IP realities. In 2016, The Republic of Ireland's Central Statistics Office (CSO) revised up GDP growth for 2015 from 7.8% to 26.3% (sic!). This extraordinary (and completely "intangible") growth had its root cause in the first inclusion of SNA 2008 IP rules. In Ireland, many international corporations maintain patent boxes due to the attractive tax rules. Different authors have concluded since that SNA rules distort true IP figures and incentivize inappropriate behaviors of both companies and policy givers.

> "The message is that the treatment of Intellectual Property according to SNA 2008 is flawed." (Lynch 2018, p 1)

Bound to IFRS rules and commercial accounting standards, we need to treat SNA IP data with caution. However, they provide the only reliable source for global IP creation.

We therefore estimate INTELLECTUAL PROPERTY (like the other components of produced capital) from PPP-corrected PWT 9.1. by projection of OECD produced capital composition (Fig. 10). World Inc. thus books 20.76 tn USD as INTELLECTUAL PROPERTY.

Any potential governmental portion of this IP cannot be separated. In accordance with SNA and literature, we need to assume that the whole IP is generated by companies. Therefore, this value is included in the total intangible value booked after the acquisition of all companies. We assume the INTELLECTUAL PROPERTY share of INTANGIBLE ASSETS to be equally distributed between listed companies, SMEs and SOEs, and correct GOODWILL downward accordingly to avoid double counting.

8

Liability consolidation

In a technical accounting sense, the booking of GOODWILL in 7.3 can be understood as the result of transactional acquisitions of all companies globally. It can also be understood as the balance sheet consolidation result of the asset class Equity.

Equity is a bivalent asset. It shows up on the asset side of the shareholder as well as the liability side of the company. However, it does not nullify after global consolidation, since valuation is different. Whereas equity on the balance sheet of the shareholder is valued at market price, it is valued much lower (e.g., at nominal value) in the balance sheet of the company. The huge GOODWILL can be understood as the difference between these two valuations.

Principally and theoretically, the same outcome is possible during the consolidation of each other bivalent asset class. We will examine this in this chapter.

8.1   DEBT

Total global debt is reported neither by SNA nor by first-tier sources. It is, however, monitored by several institutions of the

Financial Services Industry, which results in an overall acceptable data quality. We use the Institute of International Finance (IIF) as the primary source. In their recent report (Tiftik and Mahmood 2019), IIF concludes that the global total debt at the end of 2018 has been 244 tn USD. This figure includes all debt types and debtor groups.

World Inc. acquires all this debt twice, from the lenders at market price, and from the debtors at book or nominal value. After the acquisition of all debt for market prices, World Inc. resolves all these liabilities. The question is whether a positive or negative consolidation value may remain on World Inc.'s balance sheet. This could happen if the consolidated view of all creditors leads to a different total value estimation than the consolidated view of all debtors.

Systematic differences between both views may have two reasons. The first reason is a systematic change in risk-free debt valuation based on interest rate movements. This may have an impact here. During the last few years, a certain asset inflation has been observed, driven by average lower interest rates, thus leading to higher valuations of some debt types. To analyze this in detail cannot be, however, the objective of this study. In a long-term view, interest rate fluctuations are expected to neutralize. Short-term asset inflation wins do not principally contribute to the value of World Inc.; instead, they reflect a momentary short-term market shift situation. Therefore, we have decided to assume fixed interest rates and not derive a positive consolidation value from potential market price increases for risk-free debt.

The second reason results from the default risk of the debt. The market price for debt includes a reservation for its default, which also should be reflected in the books of the lender (in form of del credere, contingency reserves, reservations, or default provisions). These provisions can be significant for bad debt or non-performing loans. Their global accumulated value reflects the market expectation for the total default value. We will call this global value "global debt default provision" for the purposes of this study. Since World Inc. does not default, it can book this global default provision as asset. From a transactional view, this would be a risk evaluation win when acquiring bad debt. From an asset type consolidation view, this is the positive difference of the book value and the market value of bad debt.

Debt and its default risk are widely discussed in the public. Interestingly, data sources for the global default provision are scarce and heterogeneous.

Since the financial crisis of 2008, central banks have been observing the amounts of non-performing loans. However, they oversee only major banks, and therefore, only a fraction of debt. Furthermore, the relatively volatile rate of non-performing loans - fluctuating around 3% in 2018 - is not directly linked to the write-downs or defaults. In most cases, non-performing loans are repaid, but with lower interest rates or prolonged terms. Detailed statistical data about effective write-downs of debt are not published by central banks, however. Thus, 3% can be assumed an upper threshold for the default risk.

The largest banks typically book corresponding reservations of around 1% in their balance sheets. Smaller banks, however, tend to have somewhat higher rates of reservations. They are also more frequently observed to accept debt of bad quality without booking sufficient reservations. Therefore, the value of 1% seems to be a lower threshold.

Financial service providers in customer credits – credit card debt, student loans, etc. – anecdotally report different default rates between 1% and 4%. Banks issuing mortgages have observed high defaults during various real estate crises, particularly in the financial crisis 2008. In normal times, however, including our reference year 2018, mortgage defaults remain small.

In total, we estimate the global average debt default risk in 2018 to 2.0%. We therefore estimate the global debt default provision to 4.88 tn USD. This value could be booked potentially by World Inc. as a risk evaluation win after debt acquisition. Technically, we would book this as Intangible asset. The name GLOBAL GOVERNANCE would be a good candidate for this new type of INTANGIBLE ASSET.

Why? At this point in the analysis, it is worthwhile to return to the World Bank studies about the "Wealth of Nations". In their 2018 study, the World Bank consolidated all global cross-border debt (foreign debt) to "net foreign assets." The World Bank found the global total net foreign assets to be -4.581 tn USD, which is similar to the value we found above. The World Bank gives no convincing explanation for this:

> "Finally, at the global level the value of net foreign assets…in theory should balance to zero because every financial asset must have a matching liability. However, reporting is not complete…" (Lange, Wodon, and Carey 2018, p47).

Doubtlessly, reporting is not complete, and contains gaps. The value of more than 4 tn USD represents, however, a significant share of global foreign debt. It is questionable that lenders should track these assets with error bars of several percent accuracy only. Instead, it is reasonable to interpret this value in the light of our analysis as the global default provision for foreign debt.

Already in 4.4, we have cited the World Bank's understanding of intangible capital in their 2006 "Wealth of Nations" study:

> "The largest share [of the Wealth Of Nations], intangible capital, consists of an amalgam of human capital, governance [sic!], and other factors that are difficult to value explicitly." (World Bank 2006, XX, endnote of executive summary).

It is interesting to read that "governance" is seen as component of intangible capital without major backing by theory or literature. We lean on that understanding when recommending the asset type name GLOBAL GOVERNANCE for the net debt consolidation value.

We have decided, however, not to formally include this position in World Inc.'s balance sheet, but to report it only for the sake of information. Although the figure gives a first quantitative indication about which financial advantages a truly global governance could generate, its introduction into World Inc.'s balance sheet would violate the functional neutrality principle introduced in 3.3. When World Inc. acts as one global debtor instead of independent debtors who can default, it changes the functionality of the economy. To include this would distort the objective of the study to account for the values of the global economy as it is.

8.2 PENSIONS

World Inc. acquires all pension claims of entitled citizens (beneficiaries), as well as all pension liabilities and assets of all pension debtors – pension funds, companies, and governments matching those pension claims. As before, theoretically, the global total value of these bivalent assets should be zero, provided no systematic valuation difference between assets and liabilities takes place. This is possible, however: The integrated view of all beneficiaries about their expected pensions could differ from the integrated view of all pension debtors.

Accounting principles

Several factors influence the valuation of both, assets, and liabilities.

A first question is: what pension claims qualify as an account receivable in the sense of IFRS? Since beneficiaries are private households, no formal accounting or balance sheet creation takes place. Consequentially, no formal qualification of those claims as account receivable is conducted or documented. Furthermore, the claims are rights of very different origin and quality, depending heavily on each country's legal system and on the exact scheme provided.

Three major pension system types have developed which we use to structure this thorny issue in accordance with literature.

In "pay-as-you-go" systems employees and companies pay their contributions to a – typically governmental – pension institution. Without buying assets or building capital, this institution uses these payments directly for pensions of beneficiaries. The claims of beneficiaries are not firmly quantified, but are subject to legal changes. Therefore, claims in a "pay-as-you-go" system do not qualify as account receivable. Correspondingly, the pensions institution only balances cash flows, does not account for pension liabilities, and cannot go bankrupt. The system works comparable to a tax system: whereas people are obliged to pay, they do not acquire a tangible account receivable in return for their payment. Therefore, consolidation of the world's pay-as-you-go systems nullifies.

In "defined contribution plans" (DC) and in "defined benefit plans" (DB), employees and companies pay their contributions to a pension fund. This fund acquires assets, typically financial instruments. The returns of those assets are used to provide the payments for the beneficiaries. The fund creates balance sheets structured by individual retirement accounts, and accounts for its liabilities. Consequentially, we consider that the claims against these pension funds are accounts receivables in the sense of IFRS: The beneficiary has an enforceable claim against an institution, which is backed by assets.

In a DC plan, however, the beneficiary has no entitlement for a defined retirement income. Payments are limited to the capability of the fund to provide payments, derived from the returns of their assets. Therefore, the beneficiaries carry the risk of the pension fund's asset development. The total value of beneficiaries' claims is given by the total value of the fund's assets. Thus, the consolidation of the world's DC plans also nullifies.

In DB plans, finally, the beneficiary has an entitlement for a defined retirement income. This claim is directed against the pension fund, which is backed by the employer. This opens the possibility that the total value of these claims exceeds the total value of corresponding liabilities: pension funds can be underfunded. The remaining risk of the employer theoretically shall be reflected in its balance sheet. Under IAS 19, sponsors of DB plans have to report the difference between the fair value of assets and the liabilities of the DB plans in the statement of financial position. But not all employers are listed companies and the remaining risk of the employer to cover can be inappropriately reflected by the employers' balance sheet.

For DB pension funds, no standardized price finding mechanism exists. World Inc. therefore acquires all such pension funds at book value, as well the DB claims of beneficiaries. The total underfunding of these DB plans therefore finally shows up as a remaining liability in the balance sheet of World Inc. against the beneficiaries.

Data sources

Over the last few years, the relevance of pensions has increased and many studies have been published on the topic. Due to the falling interest rates, issues to finance retirement have risen. Consequently, in recent years, pension liabilities have increased faster than pension assets (OECD 2018a). This is interpreted as alarming, therefore fostering more publicity (World Economic Forum 2019).

Still, data provision and literature are relatively immature compared to other asset classes. This is due to several reasons.

Firstly, pensions and pension-related assets are not reported in SNA. Therefore, SNA and SNA reliant sources are not providing data of appropriate quality.

Secondly, the world's countries have different approaches to the whole subject, resulting in very different pension schemes. Pension systems, considered a part of social security, are culturally deeply-rooted only in Europe and some other wealthy countries. The majority of nations has introduced pension schemes only more recently, with more limited scopes and asset values.

Further, data aggregators and second-tier sources frequently have deviating objectives and analytical approaches. International organizations tend to focus on system stability matters or coverage of systems, therefore leaving gaps in asset accounting (European Insurance and Occupational Pensions Authority 2015). Some studies are driven by the Financial Service Industry, focused on wealth management or on specific services for pension funds (Mercer 2018). Whereas these are valid sources for assets, they tend to pay less attention to liabilities. Furthermore, many countries, which manage their nations' pension schemes outside the global capital markets, are ignored. Consequentially, few of these second-tier sources pay attention to a global differentiation between DB and other schemes, which, however, is crucial for our purposes.

Two second-tier studies form the backbone of our analysis. For our detailed country-by-country analysis, many further third-tier sources need to be taken into consideration. Due to the heterogeneity of these sources and the limited comparability of pension systems, the asset class Pensions carries a considerable accuracy risk. Fig. 14 shows the final result.

Country-by-country analysis

The OECD study "Pension market in focus" (OECD 2018a) and the Willis Towers Watson study "Global Pension Assets study 2018" (Willis Towers Watson 2018) give a broad overview about the topic.

Pensions and pension assets are globally concentrated on a relatively small group of countries. Seven countries, with pension assets of more than 1 tn USD each, represent already more than 90% of the total. The US alone commands higher pension assets than the rest of the world combined.

For some countries, OECD figures allow the calculation of underfunding of DB schemes. These countries are Denmark, Finland, Germany, Guyana, Hong Kong, Iceland, Indonesia, Liechtenstein, Luxembourg, Mexico, the Netherlands, Norway, Switzerland, the United Kingdom, and the United States. For these, we use the OECD results. For other countries, especially those with more than 0.5% of global pension assets, we have carried out a country-by-country analysis based on country-specific third-tier sources.

In Australia, DC plans are dominant; only 13% of assets are bound in DB schemes. The limited underfunding is published by ARPA (Australian Prudential Regulation Authority 2019), with good reliability.

The Brazilian pension system has three pillars. Neither the non-contributary nor the mandatory contributary system contain a DB component. But the additional voluntary private pension scheme is considered fully-funded. According to the OECD, 43% of Brazilian pensions assets belong to DB plans. The moderate underfunding is roughly estimated by Swiss Re (Swiss RE 2018).

Canada is highly-dependent on DB schemes (Willis Towers Watson 2018), which opens the possibility of major underfunding. The pension system for the public sector is well-documented (Government of Canada 2018). More difficult is the estimation of underfunding of the private pension system. We project the reasonable underfunding based on a survey of S&P/TSX 60 companies (Eisen, MacDonald, and Roberts 2017), although these companies only represent 33% of the Canadian private pension assets (Statistics Canada 2019). This introduces a certain accuracy risk. However, private underfunding accounts only for around a third of considerable Canadian total; we believe the overall estimation to be quite reliable.

China has a two-component pension system which consists of a defined benefit earnings-related pension and a mandatory defined contribution scheme (OECD 2018b). The model shows major differences to Western schemes, e.g., the presence of a provincial organization. However, the limited information provided (The state council - The People's Republic of China 2019) indicates good health of the system. Assets of 729.6 bn USD are counted and cashflow is positive with 29 bn USD annually. Therefore, we do not assume an underfunding. However, some provinces report difficulties to fund their shares of the system, and China ages quickly (Minister of Finance, The people's Republic of China and Minister of Finance, Japan 2018). Therefore, in the future the situation may deteriorate.

France nearly completely (98%) relies on pay-as-you-go schemes. Supplementary funded schemes represent the rest of pensions paid (International Actuarial Association 2018). Those, however, are DC plans. Therefore, we do not account for any French underfunding.

Country	Assets	Underfunding
Australia	1,760.1	17.9
Brazil	487.6	28.8
Canada	1,769.0	216.0
China	729.6	0.0
Denmark	721.7	-2.3
Finland	162.4	-33.4
France	278.3	0.0
Germany	270.7	-55.1
Guyana	0.3	-0.1
Hong Kong	148.3	-1.9
Iceland	40.3	6.9
Indonesia	18.8	0.3
Japan	3,054.0	3,172.0
Korea	485.9	0.0
Liechtenstein	6.1	-0.1
Luxembourg	1.9	0.0
Mexico	185.6	5.9
Netherlands	1,627.8	-140.2
Norway	42.1	-5.3
Singapore	268.4	0.0
South Africa	303.0	-29.8
Sweden	653.8	-51.6
Switzerland	1,019.7	-87.6
United Kingdom	2,903.3	217.8
United States	28,169.0	6,128.2
SUM (bn USD)	**45,107.7**	**9,386.2**

Figure 14: Pension assets and underfunding

In India, the pension system is relatively immature. About 88% of the total labor force of 472 million people are without any formal pension provision. Undoubtedly, there are some data points for the assumption of underfunding. The APY (Atal Pension Yojana), the dominant DB pension scheme, counts roughly 9.6 million subscribers. The assets under management in DB schemes, however, mount only to approximately 550 M USD (Pension Fund Regulatory & Development Authority 2018). Due to the weak data availability, we have decided not to include India in World Inc.'s pensions accounting. Any potential underfunding would be expected to decrease anyway, due to the overarching trend to DC schemes in India.

The situation in Japan is challenging. Japan is rich, has an ageing population, and their pension systems tend to operate domestically, therefore not profiting from the global financial system (World Economic Forum 2017). This is risky. The data provision, however, shows significant gaps.

It starts with major differences of OECD and Willis Towers Watson for Japan's pension assets under management—a difference of more than 1 tn USD. Our analysis shows that Japan reports only the Governmental pension investment fund (GPIF) to OECD (Government Pension Investment Fund 2017). GPIF manages the funds for the Japanese pension service (JPS), the Governmental pension scheme. However, there are also corporate pension schemes, mostly DB schemes, which are correctly included in Willis Towers Watson figures.

While Japanese pension assets can ultimately be determined, this does not apply to liabilities. A direct estimation of GPIF's underfunding is, therefore, not possible. However, JPS reports a strong negative cashflow of nearly 140 bn USD annually (Japan Pension Service 2016). This allows us to set up a funding model using data for the real investment rates of return on Japanese pension assets (OECD 2018a). According to our model, the funding gap of just the GPIF is estimated to be 2.975 tn USD.

In absolute and relative terms, the underfunding of the corporate pension system is much smaller, although still significant. Corporate pension assets reach 744 bn USD in 2018 (Nomura Research Institute 2018). Based on a 2016 analysis (Nikkei Asian

Review 2017), we project the corporate pension underfunding to 197 bn USD end of 2018.

According to our analysis, Japan's underfunding is the second largest in the world, after the US, and amounts to 3.172 tn USD. The inaccuracy risk, however, is higher than for other countries.

In South Korea, the National Pension scheme (NPS) covers mandatory as well as optional contributors (National Pension Service 2018). The National Pension Fund of South Korea is a reserve fund which finances and executes the National Pension Scheme, manages the assets, and pays benefits to the beneficiaries. Its work is documented better than in Japan, but their liabilities are not reported.

The NPS runs a minimal negative cashflow, and the fund had a negative return of minus 0.92% on his considerable capital of 485.9 bn USD in 2018. 2018 was, however, the first year with negative returns, caused by turbulences at the financial markets. It is not clear yet if this situation describes a temporary issue or if a serious funding gap might be underlying. In any case, figures would be small. We have decided not to assign an evident underfunding to Korea.

Singapore's retirement income system is based on the Central Provident Fund (CPF) (Mercer 2018). It covers all Singaporean and permanent resident workers earning a monthly wage of at least 50 SGD. The CPF is a DC scheme (OECD 2018b). Therefore, the CPF cannot be underfunded in terms of our definition. The pension system in Singapore is regarded to have no underfunding.

In South Africa, the public sector is dominated by DB plans. The Government Employees Pension Fund (GEPF) is a DB fund, in which all employees of national and provincial government are enrolled. Its assets and assets of other funds are managed by the Public investment corporation (PIC). According to the latest available report of the PIC, the GEPF is one of the few fully funded DB pension funds. It owns assets of 216 bn USD, and is funded with 116% (Public Investment Corporation 2018). Since the private sector is dominated by DC plans, we do not assume that the private pensions change this positive picture.

The Pension system in Sweden consists mainly of the guaranteed pension, the income-based old age pension, and occupational pensions. The tax financed guaranteed pension (Ministry of Health and Social Affairs 2016) cannot be underfunded with respect to our definition.

The income-based old age pension consists of the Income pension, a pay-as-you-go system, and of the premium pension, a fully funded DC plan. The so-called ATP, a DB scheme, is still a part of the income based old age pension (Swedish Pensions Agency 2018). However, the trend is shifting to DC plans and the old ATP schemes are wearing out.

According to the Orange Report, covering the national income-based pension (including ATP), in 2018 pension assets exceeded pension liabilities by 52 bn USD (Swedish Pensions Agency 2018). Thus, ATP and income-based pension are adequately financed.

The occupational pension system in Sweden mainly consists of DC plans and has a positive cashflow of 7.6 billion USD at the end of 2018 (Sundberg 2018; Swedish Pensions Agency 2018). This signals a properly funded pension system, too, although neither data about the share of DB plans nor about pension liabilities in occupational pension schemes are provided.

In total, underfunding of pensions accrues to 9.386 tn USD. This is the remaining pension obligation of World Inc., a net financial asset of the beneficiaries.

8.3   OTHER LIABILITIES

Fig. 3 lists further bivalent asset types that World Inc. consolidates. Investments in Financial assets > 1 yr. are included in 9.1. Investments in Associates and Joint Ventures (JV) have been recognized in 7.3. Current bivalent assets and current liabilities are considered to nullify; there is no major obvious reason why valuation of these assets should vary significantly between asset and liability view. Loans payable are included in 9.1. The same happens with deferred tax liabilities; they nullify during the acquisition of governments. Other non-current liabilities are resolved the same way.

Therefore, for the purposes of this study, we can assume all other liabilities to nullify during consolidation. No remaining asset values are booked.

9

Money

World Inc. acquires all CASH AND CASH EQUIVALENTS, all money, and all central banks. The outcome of the corresponding balance sheet consolidation decisively depends on the nature of the individual asset as monovalent or bivalent asset.

9.1 ACCOUNTING PRINCIPLES

From a balance sheet point of view, different kinds of money are used. Historically, money started as commodity money. Commodities - barley, wheat, livestock, for instance - can be used for trade. They also fulfil the traditional three functions of money: as a medium of exchange, as a store of value, and as a unit of account. Commodity money is monovalent money: truly produced and created on the asset side of the issuer's balance sheet. Gold, silver, and copper are commodities, too. Gold and silver currencies, thus commodity currencies dominated the money landscape in the last 2,000 years until quite recently.

Nowadays, however, the money landscape is dominated by fiat money. The Latin word *fiat* (meaning: "Let there be!") is reminiscent of Vulgate, the Latin version of the Bible. When God created the world on day one, he started with the creation of light: "Fiat lux! (Let there be light!)."

Fiat currencies are not created by God, still they are created *ex nihilo* – out of nothing. The granting institution, the Central Bank, just declares the money valuable. In the language of balance sheet accounting, the money is created on the liability side of the Central Bank and transferred to the asset side of a lender. The resulting asset, therefore, is bivalent. Fiat money is bivalent money.

Just recently, science noticed that the nature of money as monovalent or bivalent is critical, and that the exact counterpart of "fiat money" had not yet been described.

In Germany, Austria, and Switzerland specifically, some authors have referred to the Austrian school of economics, to Friedrich Hayek, and others. They have developed alternative money systems based on monovalent money (Mayer 2015, 2017). This monovalent money is called "Aktivgeld". (An established English translation does not exist yet. "Asset money" might be an acceptable candidate, used in this study. The English expression "active money" is something different, it refers to the total amount of money in circulation.) "Aktivgeld" is truly produced and is created on the asset side of a balance sheet. This school of thinking has also influenced the Swiss initiative "Vollgeld", which strived to change the money system in Switzerland. After a broad public discourse on the matter, the initiative finally failed to convince the Swiss electorate in 2018.

This discourse has made obvious that the category monovalent money (asset money) is not exhausted by commodity money. There are further types of asset money. Cyber currencies, for example, are asset money too. In the absence of a granting institution, Bitcoin and other cyber currencies draw their value from the fact that they cannot be produced *ex nihilo*. They are produced at a cost that reflects their intrinsic value.

All types of asset money are monovalent assets. They will show up in World Inc.'s balance sheet as CASH AND CASH EQUIVALENTS.

9.2   FIAT MONEY

Currently, all national currencies are fiat currencies. Some service providers monitor them. WhatCurrency lists 253 national fiat currencies in detail (WhatCurrency.net 2019). Specifically, all major trade currencies (USD, EUR, GBP, JPY, CNY, CHF) are fiat currencies. Whereas asset money is not restricted to commodity money, fiat money is not restricted to national currencies. Facebook's project Libra is an example for a private fiat currency.

All fiat money is acquired twice by World Inc. - as asset and as liability. Since fiat currencies fulfill the money function "store of value," no valuation differences exist between the asset and the liability view of a fiat currency. Thus, all fiat currencies nullify.

No remaining asset is booked by World Inc. after acquisition of the world's fiat currencies.

9.3   MONOVALENT MONEY

Monovalent money (asset money) is acquired once by World Inc., and thus, it is activated. Different kinds of asset money are taken into consideration.

Monetary gold

Gold can be used for different purposes, and therefore, is booked in different asset types. SNA defines the accounting standards for gold, which are used also for this work (United Nations et al. 2011). Gold as an interim product of industry – e.g., for jewelry – is booked as inventories, therefore it has been included in COMMERCIAL INVENTORIES (6.4). The final durable product, e.g., jewelry, is accounted for as CONSUMER DURABLES (6.4). MONETARY GOLD, however, stored by central banks and financial institutions, is considered a financial asset by SNA. Since monetary gold is the only monovalent asset in this category, it needs to be accounted for separately here; it is not yet included in another account.

As of December 31, 2018, the world's central banks had gold reserves of 34,214.06 tons, and gold has been valued at 1,279.00 USD/troy ounce (World Gold Council 2019). This results in MONETARY GOLD RESERVES of 1.41 tn USD.

Private investments, conducted via SPDR funds, receive the same accounting treatment. (United Nations et al. 2011). The total funds holding volume is significantly lower than the Central Bank reserves, however (2,449.90 tons on 31st of December 2018) (World Gold Council 2019). In total the position GOLD SPDR HOLDINGS accounts for 100.7 bn USD only.

Crypto currencies

More than hundred crypto currencies are traded on different platforms. Bitcoin still dominates the asset category in terms of market capitalization. Several financial institutions monitor this market; we use the data of CoinMarketCap (CoinMarketCap 2019). The total value of CRYPTO CURRENCIES is still limited. As of December 31, 2018, the category was 128.4 bn USD.

10

Synthesis

10.1 WORLD INC. BALANCE SHEET

After iteration through all asset classes now the balance sheet of World Inc. can be assembled (Fig. 15).

In total, World Inc. has spent 687.53 tn USD for the acquisition of the world's assets, approximately 8 times annual GDP (85.79 tn USD (2014) in 2018). A few observations:

- LAND value is strongly concentrated. 65% of land's value is represented by less than 1 M km² URBAN LAND. Given the huge relative value of URBAN LAND, tangible statistical data as well as scientific discussion are underrepresented. Although agricultural land – CROPLAND and PASTURE LAND – still accounts for 32.2% of the land's value, its overall role as a major production factor is limited. The rest of the world's land - more than 65% of the total by area - only accounts for 3.69 tn USD, 2.8% by value. This value concentration has increased in the last few years. It is reflected by huge price gradients per km², depending on land type and service.

World Inc Balance Sheet December 31, 2018 (in tn USD)	
Assets	**687.53**
Fixed assets	**638.99**
Property	**184.01**
Land	132.09
Cropland	26.45
Pasture land	16.06
Forest	2.69
Barren land	1.00
Urban land	85.89
Subsoil assets	51.91
Oil	30.79
Gas	3.73
Coal	6.85
Minerals (10)	10.54
Plant	**260.27**
Dwellings	119.84
Other buildings	140.43
Equipment	**50.73**
Commercial equipment	41.98
Military equipment	8.74
Intangible Assets	**143.99**
Goodwill	117.63
Listed companies, disclosed	8.00
Listed companies, acquired	35.92
SMEs, acquired	72.73
SOEs, acquired	0.99
Intellectual property	20.76
Brand value, licenses	5.60
(Global Governance)	(4.88)
Current assets	**48.54**
Inventories	**46.90**
Commercial inventories	17.54
Consumer durables	29.36
Cash and cash equivalents	**1.64**
Monetary gold reserves	1.41
Gold SPDR holdings	0.10
Crypto currencies	0.13
Liabilities and Equity	**687.53**
Unfunded pension liabilities	9.39
Share capital	678.14

Figure 15:   World Inc. Balance Sheet

- These price gradients strongly drive conversion from relatively cheap land types into more valuable ones. All land types are utilized for conversion into urban land, which drives urban sprawl. The conversion of wood into agricultural land is also heavily incentivized. Why forests are burned and cleared, is quite obvious, therefore. Also protected areas are clearly under economic pressure to be converted into agricultural land.

- Overexploitation and environmental pollution have already affected some land's asset values, and continue to do so. The fishing revenues of the seas are not covering costs any more. Additionally, the value of FOREST has decreased noticeably.

- SUBSOIL ASSETS are still relatively cheap. OIL represents the by far largest share of their value (59.3%). The low relative value of MINERALS makes it attractive to bring new raw materials to the surface of the Earth, instead of recycling the old atoms of copper, iron, and silver which well may end up as waste or environmental pollution. The development of the last years does not indicate major changes of the existing economic models. Coal, however, is in decline.

- Tangible assets such as PLANT, EQUIPMENT, and INVENTORIES represent about half of World Inc.'s total assets. Buildings (PLANT) are very concentrated, especially in cities in advanced economies. Their value has increased in the last few years, driven by construction and investments, but also by price increases (asset inflation). The latter is potentially not fully reflected in the numbers.

- The value of chattels of all kind is reflected in EQUIPMENT and in INVENTORIES. Chattels tend to be accounted for inhomogeneously and patchily; theoretical depth of literature is limited. This mainstream treatment of these assets reflects their perceived limited importance as production factors. Still they total to 97.63 tn USD. They play a major role for supply chains, and for the economic well-being of households and of governments.

- INTANGIBLE ASSETS account for 143.99 tn USD, more than the world's land. This is very significant. Further, INTANGIBLE ASSETS may still be underreported. They form a challenge for economic theory. These assets are intangible, but nevertheless real. They are monovalent assets which cannot be created *ex nihilo* and are part of real economy. World Inc. needed to pay more than 100 tn USD over their book value for the world's 200-300 M companies. But what value exactly does this GOODWILL represent? And what exactly is the theoretical foundation for the well-defined 4.88 tn USD we have earmarked as GLOBAL GOVERNANCE? Quality of statistical data and scientific activity are not yet in line with the significance of this asset class.

- Like the hound of the Baskervilles, some asset categories frequently bark despite being absent. DEBT is irrelevant on a global level. All economic activity happens and is funded in the present. There is nothing like a burden for future generations; this is just a popular illusion. Given the relatively low value of 4.88 tn USD for the global debt default risk, it seems that debt and "debt crises" may be a bit overvalued by politics, media and public.

- Fiat currencies are at the heart of political economy. They are further in the focus of merchants, and at the heart of commercial accounting. However, they are not part of the real economy. They do not leave a footprint in World Inc.'s balance sheet.

- Although monovalent asset money (gold and crypto currencies) forms an interesting theoretical challenger for the fiat currency world, it reflects only a relatively small value, yet.

10.2 BALANCE SHEET OF HUMANKIND

In Chapter 4.5, we introduced the Balance Sheet of Humankind (Fig. 6) to achieve a total view of the assets of the world, and to crosscheck the findings within World Inc.'s balance sheet by an independent method.

Human Capital

Since humans are not the property of a state or of a company, human capital rests with humankind and cannot be transferred to World Inc. Consequentially, human capital is not subject of commercial accounting and is not covered by IFRS rules.

Additionally, SNA does not provide rules for human capital accounting, or reports on human capital. This is quite an interesting observation, because economic theory knows since centuries that human labor is a core value driver. Although Karl Marx had propelled this idea, it is not a primarily socialist concept. Instead, its reception by economic mainstream theory is much older; Adam Smith had already seen the core value of human labor.

There is no binding global framework to account for human capital yet.

Two approaches have emerged, however. One approach (the "input approach") focuses on investments into human capital, with special interest in education. A major objective is to analyze tangible returns on education services (e.g., schools, universities), and other related public functions. A financial value can then be attributed to these services. This school of thinking is important when economically rationalizing levels of public spending and public policies. The method struggles, however, with different valuations of private and public spending, with exits from human capital (deaths, retirements), and the heterogeneity of measurement principles in detail.

The second approach ("output approach"), introduced already in the 90s (Jorgenson and Fraumeni 1992), treats humans as factor of production comparable to other assets. This school of thinking defines HUMAN CAPITAL as the present value of the labor income of an individual. This methodological approach has widely succeeded in economic studies. Therefore, data situation and literature are relatively best. We follow this approach to estimate the humankind's HUMAN CAPITAL.

The World Bank has an excellent global know-how base for human capital, probably second to none. The World Bank operates, firstly, the specific "Human Capital Project" (World Bank 2019), which studies the impact of input factors in detail like education, health services, and gender differences. The "Human Capital Project" is the dominant global think tank for human capital studies and policy advisory with focus on the input approach.

The World Bank also masters the economic side and the output approach. Their 2018 "Wealth of Nations" study works intensively about the world's HUMAN CAPITAL and claims:

> "Although the recognition of the importance of human capital wealth is not new..., this study is the first to provide measures of human capital wealth worldwide based on a time series of household surveys." (Lange, Wodon, and Carey 2018, p136).

In fact, the World Bank has undertaken enormous efforts to assemble a valid and homogeneous global database for this study. Household surveys were conducted in 141 countries. These surveys have been used to construct a set of matrices that capture (1) the probability that individuals are working depending on their age, sex, and years of education, and (2) their likely earnings when working, again, by age, sex, and years of schooling. The World Bank's International Income Distribution Database of household and labor force surveys could be leveraged to fill data gaps in specific countries. This groundbreaking work dwarfs previous analyses, which had been restricted to certain countries or social groups mainly.

Despite the detailed work, the World Bank's figures are, of course, exposed to major drivers of inaccuracy. Most important are the assumptions about the long-term future of wage development. Constant or moderately growing GDPs are assumed. And the World Bank assumes a discount rate of -1.5% globally in all countries. This discount rate d is given as (Eq. 11):

$$1+d = \left(1+g\right)/\left(1+r\right)$$

With: g real wage growth rate and

    r return rate on capital (as before).

On a country-by-country base, this contrasts with the constancy of r used in all other capital types by the World Bank, introducing a country-by-country distortion for the capital relations. And on a global base, the sensitivity of HUMAN CAPITAL for d is high. All this gives the HUMAN CAPITAL figures a relatively high accuracy risk.

Still, World Bank data, referring to 2014, are unrivaled in quality. We use them in our study, and project them to 2018.

Although the World Bank's human capital study covers 141 countries, this list is not completely exhaustive. Some relevant countries are not covered, e.g., North Korea, Iran, Cuba, Czech Republic, Serbia. Of course, also many minor and many poor countries are not included. The countries out of scope have, in total, 506.3 M inhabitants (2018), 6.7% of the world's population. The World Bank assigns no human capital to those countries and those people. Instead, the World Bank totals the human capital of 141 countries to 738.8 tn USD (2014).

We are not following the World Bank in fully neglecting these "Rest of World" countries. These 506.3 M people contribute to the world's human capital, obviously. The World Bank assigns every country to an economically defined subgroup ("high income," "upper middle income," and so on). Also, each of the "Rest of World" countries are assigned to such subgroup. For each of these subgroups, a mean HUMAN CAPITAL per capita can be calculated. In absence of a country specific HUMAN CAPITAL value for the "Rest of World" countries we use the average of the according subgroup as estimation for the country's HUMAN CAPITAL per capita. This allows us to estimate the HUMAN CAPITAL for the Rest of World. For 2014 we find it as 12.1 tn USD, after all 1.6% of the world's total HUMAN CAPITAL. Therefore, based on World Bank figures, we estimate the total HUMAN CAPITAL for 2014 as 750.9 tn USD.

During the last decades, HUMAN CAPITAL per capita has increased continuously, although somewhat less than GDP per capita. Differences between countries are large. Particularly middle-income countries have progressed, whereas many poor countries have only started to catch up recently (Fig. 16). High-income OECD countries have increased their HUMAN CAPITAL per capita least, according to the World Bank.

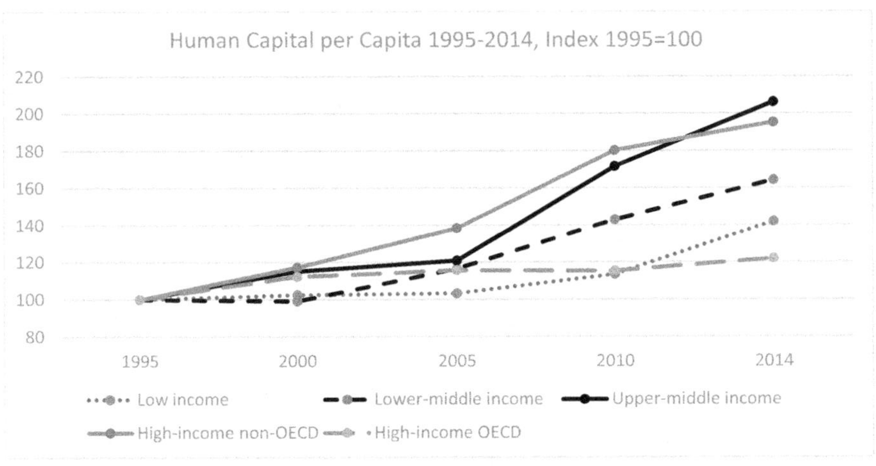

Figure 16:   Human Capital development 1995-2014 (Source: World Bank)

The GDP growth in the time 2014–2018 has been in line with the period 2010-2014. The quite steady increase of HUMAN CAPITAL per capita allows us to project human capital for 2018 by a linear extrapolation of HUMAN CAPITAL per capita. We extrapolate on a country-by-country basis, and use linear regression with over-weight for the most recent four years 2010-2014 for each country. Population per country is available by different sources until 2018. For consistency purposes, we use World Bank data.

We find, that during the four years 2014-2018 the world's HUMAN CAPITAL has grown by 59.0 tn USD to 809.9 tn USD in 2018. This growth equals a compound annual growth rate (CAGR) of 1.91%, which is explained partly (with 1.15%) by population growth, and with 0.75% by HUMAN CAPITAL growth per capita. This only modest overall per capita development is driven by the ageing and stagnant high-income countries, which still make up the lion's share of global HUMAN CAPITAL.

Consumption

In Chapter 4.5 we derived that the liability of humankind equals the net present value of its consumption. Whereas human capital still lacks standardization of accounting rules, consumption is defined in the SNA framework (United Nations et al. 2011). Since governments and their assets have been acquired by World Inc., also governmental consumption needs to be funded with the world's total assets. Thus, we define CONSUMPTION for this study as the present value of "final consumption expenditure" in the sense of SNA 2008.

Based on SNA data, integrated global consumption data are available via various global data integrators. These data, however, are ex post data. The projection models for future consumption are less well developed. Household consumption behaves similar to HUMAN CAPITAL: Future consumption of a person depends not only on current consumption level, but also on age, gender, education, and life expectancy. In an ideal world, future household consumption could be modeled along a differentiated matrix model like the one the World Bank has developed for HUMAN CAPITAL.

The World Bank is indeed working on it. The World Bank Project "Global Consumption database" (The World Bank Group - www.worldbank.org 2015) provides detailed data about consumption patterns per country, based on household surveys and demographic structural data. However, these data refer to the year 2010 latest, and do not yet allow projections into the future.

Therefore, the projection of present consumption into the future needs to be conducted in this study via a classical NPV approach, comparable to other asset classes and in accordance with literature (World Bank 2011).

For the estimation of present annual global consumption, we use World Bank data as major source. Consumption in 2017 has been 62.62 tn USD (2014). More than 100 countries have already submitted their 2018 data, which allows a projection of the world's 2018 consumption based on these figures. We estimate the 2018 consumption to 64.78 tn USD (2014). Average annual growth in the time 2014…2018 has been 2.74% in constant currencies.

In Chapter 4.5 we saw that the World Bank (World Bank 2011) estimates the capital value of Household Consumption based on work of Hamilton and Hartwick (Hamilton and Hartwick 2005), as per Eq. (1):

$$W_t = NPV\left(C(t)\right) = \sum_{i=t}^{t+T-1} \frac{C(i)}{(1+\rho)^{i-t}}$$

Where:

W_t is the total value of wealth, or capital, in year t;

$C(i)$ is consumption in year i;

ρ is the pure rate of time preference;

T is the consumption time (in years).

We follow the World Bank in assuming that the pure rate of time preference ρ =1.5%, in accordance with older literature (Pearce 1999). This simplification, however, introduces an accuracy risk in accordance with our previous remarks about canonized discount factors (4.4). In the absence of a detailed profile or model for every citizen's future consumption we also follow the World Bank to project constant 25 years of future consumption for the NPV, thus setting T=25.

The World Bank assumes the future consumption level to be constant. This assumption rests on older models by Solow (1974, 1986). However, this simplification is neither consistent with the statistical observation – consumption grows – nor with the theoretical work of Hamilton and Hartwick the World Bank cites, but only partially uses. Unused by the World Bank, Hamilton and Hartwick derive their Proposition 1 (Eq. 12):

$$\dot{C} = rG - \dot{G}$$

Where:

$\dot{C}$ is the time derivative of consumption C;

G is the net investment,

$\dot{G}$ is the time derivative of net investment;

r is the return rate on capital (as before).

Therefore, future consumption levels are correlated with investment and thus changes of capital levels. We respect this correlation, and project future consumption with a constant growth rate c.

Integration

This allows us to finalize the Balance Sheet of Humankind (Fig. 17).

Balance Sheet of Humankind December 31, 2018 (in tn USD)	
Assets	**1,497.46**
Human capital	809.94
World Inc pensions	9.39
World Inc equity	678.14
Liabilities and Equity	**1,497.46**
Consumption (@1,13% CAGR)	1,497.46

Figure 17:   Balance Sheet of Humankind

The total assets of humankind, 1,497.46 tn USD (2014), consisting of HUMAN CAPITAL and World Inc.'s assets, are sufficient to fund the CONSUMPTION of humankind with a future annual growth rate of c = 1.13%. This is less than the average annual growth rate of the last years (2014…2018) of 2.74%.

To support that growth rate of 2.74% in the mid-term future, humankind would require 1,884.92 tn USD total assets. Eq. (12) hints as to why it may prove to be difficult to maintain this consumption growth: r is set as 4% and falling. High increases of consumption are only possible due to divestments, particularly depletion of natural resources. As shown in Chapter 5, the value of subsoil resources is limited, however, and some further asset types (FOREST, seas) are already shrinking. Therefore, a projection of 2.74% consumption growth for the next 25 years seems overly optimistic. 1,884.92 tn USD mark an upper limit for the plausible total assets.

On the other hand, constant future consumption, following the World Bank's 2006 methodology, would require only 1,358.84 tn USD (2014). In 2006, World Bank could not identify 78% of the assets required for that time's consumption projection. Here, we see no capital gaps anymore; constant consumption is more than covered. Constant consumption marks, therefore, a lower limit for the plausible total assets.

The wide range of future CONSUMPTION projections demonstrates the limits of the methodology. We conclude: The confidence range for the humankind's total assets ranks from 1,350 – 1,880 tn USD (2014). With 1,497.46 tn USD (2014) we find ourselves in this range.

Given the many inaccuracy drivers we mentioned, we come to the conclusion that the recovery rate is satisfactory. Within confidence limits, the results of our study look reasonable and reliable. No major capital gaps remain, and both balance sheets are truly balanced.

10.3 WORLD BALANCE SHEET

Formally, World Inc.'s balance sheet and the Balance Sheet of Humankind can be brought into one consolidated World Balance Sheet (Fig. 1). The liability positions PENSIONS and EQUITY in the Balance Sheet of World Inc. (Fig. 15) are resolved with the corresponding positions of the Balance Sheet of Humankind (Fig. 17).

Outlook

The difficulty lies not in the new ideas, but
in escaping from the old ones.
(J. M. KEYNES)

Due to the broad scope of our work, we have touched upon several theoretical construction pillars of economic theory and have found some weak spots. Managing the world's assets properly in the future will require some investments in theory and practical accounting tools.

Firstly, political economics and business economics have sometimes different views on the same topics. To treat governmental purchases as consumption in principle is misleading. The treatment in accounting should not depend on the actor but on the asset. The same holds true for purchases of consumers. Governments should accelerate the implementation of balance sheets, e.g., of SALM framework, and improve their asset management accordingly. SNA and commercial frameworks like IFRS should be harmonized, when it comes to basic concepts and asset definitions.

Also, money theory seems to have room for improvement. It is an interesting observation that World Inc. could technically acquire all assets globally without a dime of own capital. The only requirement was the support of a central bank that controls a fiat currency (see 3.3).

Undoubtedly, the historic development from pure commodity money to pure fiat money has been a long one. One major early milestone was the introduction of minted coins. Already at that time the nominal value of the coin exceeded the metal value by a certain (limited) margin (the "seigniorage"). The invention of paper money marked a further important milestone on this road. However, it is fair to say that the end of Bretton Woods system, not earlier than 1973, has brought the final breakthrough for the global reign of pure fiat currencies. Money theory has not much reacted to the 1973 groundbreaking change in money value fundaments, yet.

Shortly after 1973, in step with other reforms of the Reagan era, the balance sheet of the FED began to grow considerably. Is it accidental that the world's wealth has started to distribute more unevenly than before around this time? Or could already other major acquirers make use of the financing mechanism of World Inc., accumulating monovalent assets in exchange for bivalent ones, which finally nullify? The widely used central bank mechanism of quantitative easing deserves a deeper analysis, and a better theoretical justification.

Also, value theory has come in our spotlight. This deserves a broader view.

Asset classes in World Inc.'s balance sheet are real assets, they exist. Particularly, they cannot be created *ex nihilo*, they are part of real economy. In contrast to this, financial assets – fiat money, debt, most noticeably - have nullified. The difference between monovalent assets and bivalent assets is obviously fundamental, yet not appropriately reflected by value theory. One reason may be, that this value theory is centuries old and has historically grown.

More than 300 years ago, when the first steps into national accounting were taken, the Physiocrats dominated the economic thinking. They thought that agricultural land was the principal source of all value. Even if this theory should have complied with that time's agrarian economic model: Now, it is obsolete. Agricultural land – CROPLAND and PASTURE LAND – account for 2.8% of the world's total capital only.

100 years later, the classical economists beginning with Adam Smith put industrial production in the center of their value theory. "Produced capital" was born, still being in the center of SNA accounting today. PLANT, EQUIPMENT, and INVENTORIES were the capital of the 19ᵗʰ century's capitalist, beyond LAND. But also "produced capital" today accounts for 23.9% of total assets only.

Karl Marx then pushed the already older idea that labor would be the principal value. His thinking referred to the mature industrialized world, reflecting today's reality obviously better: Finally, HUMAN CAPITAL represents more than 50% of the world's total assets. Interesting still, that HUMAN CAPITAL has not made it into international accounting standards, until now. But the role of HUMAN CAPITAL is already declining; other capital forms are progressing quickly. The high time of mature industrialism seems to be over. INTANGIBLE ASSETS are already significant. They account, as of today, for 9.6% of the total capital, 20.9% of the commercial assets, and grow.

However, INTANGIBLE ASSETS are badly understood and only patchily reported. The difference between market capitalization and book value is monovalent and as such a real value. So what value is incorporated in the huge GOODWILL exactly, on a collective level?

Where are the capital theories for the post-industrialized world, substantiating yet vague concepts like INTANGIBLE ASSETS or GOODWILL? What, if not land, produced capital, and labor, are the production factors of the digital society, the knowledge society, the green society?

Beyond the work of WorldBalanceSheet.org., there is no institutionalization of the concept of integrated global capital monitoring, unfortunately. Institutionalized statistics today have an overall conservative effect. The SNA is an insular political creation of international governments, dissolved from underlying commercial reality, and reflecting outdated theoretical foundations. It does not seem to have much momentum of modernization. Born at the beginning of the Cold War, it is a 20th century management tool for a Hobbesian world of competing nations.

The SNA deserves a major overhaul, with focus on capital management. It should be supported by a powerful truly global agency. This shift could provide the data it takes for the global economic management of the World.

It would underpin the 21st century vision of a Kantian world of United Nations to manage the joint resources of our planet.

12

References

Alba, Ruben. 2014. *2014 SBA Fact Sheet Norway*: OECD.

Amico, Alissa. 2012. *Corporate Reporting of Intangible Assets: A Progress Report. Report for the OECD Corporate Governance Committee meeting, 18-20 April 2012*: OECD.

Anderson, Patrick L. 2009. "The Value of Private Businesses in the United States." *Business Economics*, 44(2): 87–108.

Arya, Neeraj. 2017. *SMEs Role in Indian Manufacturing*: India Brand Equity Foundation.

Aschauer, David A. 1989. "Is public expenditure productive?" *Journal of monetary economics*, 23(2): 177–200.

Aschauer, David A. 2000. "Public Capital and Economic Growth: Issues of Quantity, Finance, and Efficiency." *Economic Development and Cultural Change*, 48(2): 391–406.

Australian Prudential Regulation Authority. 2019. "Statistics. Quarterly Superannuation Performance."

Bank for International Settlement. 2019. Residential and Commercial property prices. https://www.bis.org/statistics/pp_commercial.htm?m=6%7C288%7C646 (accessed July 25, 2019).

Bookman, Joice, and et al. 2010. *Small and Medium-Sized Enterprises: Characteristics and Performance. Investigation No. 332-510; USITC Publication 4189*: United States International Trade Commission.

BP. 2019. *Full report – BP Statistical Review of World Energy 2019.*

Brandmeir, Kathrin, Michaela Grimm, Michael Heise, and Arne Holzhausen. 2018. *Allianz Global Wealth Report 2018*: Allianz Economic Research.

British Geological Survey. 2019. World mineral statistics data. http://www.bgs.ac.uk/mineralsuk/statistics/wms.cfc?-method=searchWMS (accessed July 16, 2019).

Burger, Nicholas, C. Chazali, G. Gaduh, and et al. 2015. *Reforming Policies for Small and Medium-Sized Enterprises in Indonesia*: RAND Corporation.

Cangoz, M. C., Sebastien Boitreaud, and Christopher Dychala. 2018. "World Bank Policy Research Paper WPS 8624: How Do Countries Use an Asset and Liability Management Approach? A survey on Sovereign Balance Sheet Management." *World Bank Treasury.*

CapGemini. 2018. *World Wealth Report.*

CoinMarketCap. 2019. Kryptowährung Marktkapitalisierungen. https://coinmarketcap.com/de/ (accessed September 16, 2019).

Datta, Madhusudan. 2006. "Measurement of Capital Stock: The PIM and the Equivalent Proportional Depreciation Approach." *Indian Economic Review, New Series*, Vol. 41(No 2): 173–94.

Department of Statistics Malaysia. 2019. Small and Medium Enterprises (SME) Performance 2018. https://www.dosm.gov.my (accessed September 9, 2019).

Doss, Cheryl, Caitlin Kieran, and Talip Kilic. 2017. *Measuring Ownership, Control, and Use of Assets. World Bank Policy Research Working Paper WPS 8146*: World Bank Group.

Eisen, Colie, David MacDonald, and Chris Roberts. 2017. "The Lion's Share. Pension deficits and shareholder payments among Canada's largest companies." *Canadian Centre for Policy Alternatives (CCPA).*

El-Barmelgy, Mohamed M., Ahmad M. Shalaby, A. N. Usama, and M. A. Shaimaa. 2014. "Economic Land Use Theory and Land Value in Value Model." *International Journal of Economics and Statistics*, 2: 91–98.

European Insurance and Occupational Pensions Authority. 2015. "Financial Stability Report."

European Union. 2003. Commission Recommendation of 6 May 2003 concerning the definition of micro, small and medium-sized enterprises. EUR-Lex - 32003H0361 - EN - EUR-Lex. https://eur-lex.europa.eu/legal-content/EN/TXT/?uri=CELEX:32003H0361 (accessed July 10, 2019).

Eurostat. 2018. *Statistics on small and medium-sized enterprises - Statistics Explained*: Eurostat.

Eurostat. 2019. Home - Eurostat. https://ec.europa.eu/eurostat/ (accessed July 4, 2019).

FAOSTAT. 2019. FAOSTAT provides free access to food and agriculture data for over 245 countries and territories and covers all FAO regional groupings from 1961 to the most recent year available. http://www.fao.org/faostat/en/#home (accessed July 19, 2019).

Feenstra, Robert C., Robert Inklaar, and Marcel P. Timmer. 2015. "The Next Generation of the Penn World Table." *American Economic Review*, 105(10): 3150–82.

Gadzinski, Gregory, Markus Schuller, and Andrea Vacchino. 2016. "The Global Capital Stock. A Proxy for the Unobservable Global Market Portfolio." *SSRN Electronic Journal.*

Government of Canada. 2018. "Public Accounts of Canada 2018. Summary Report and Consolidated Financial Statements."

Government Pension Investment Fund. 2017. "Annual Report Fiscal Year 2017."

Gupta, Sanjeev, Alvar Kangur, Chris Papageorgiou, and Abdoul Wane. 2014. "Efficiency-Adjusted Public Capital and Growth." *World Development*, 57: 164–78.

Haigh, David, Teresa de Lemus, Angel Alloza, Alex Haigh, and Annabel Brown. 2018. *Brand Finance GIFT 2018. Global Intangible Finance Tracker (GIFT) 2018 - an annual review of the world's intangible value*: Brand Finance.

Hamilton, Kirk, and John M. Hartwick. 2005. "Investing Exhaustible Resource Rents and the Path of Consumption." *The Canadian Journal of Economics*, Vol. 38(No 2): 615–21.

IFPRI. 2019. Global Futures and Strategic Foresight. IMPACT Model. http://www.ifpri.org/program/impact-model (accessed July 24, 2019).

IFRS. 2019. IAS 38 — Intangible Assets. https://www.iasplus.com/en/standards/ias/ias38 (accessed September 3, 2019).

IMF. 2017. *Estimating the stock of public capital in 170 countries. Jan 2017 update*: IMF.

IMF. 2019. IMF DataMapper. https://www.imf.org/external/data-mapper/datasets (accessed July 4, 2019).

Innovation, Science and Economic Development Canada. 2019. *Key Small Business Statistics January 2019*: Minister of Industry Canada.

International Actuarial Association. 2018. "Defined Benefit Pension plan: Funding and the Role of Actuaries."

International Energy Agency. 2018. *World energy statistics 2018.* Paris: IEA.

Japan Pension Service. 2016. "Annual Report 2016."

Jorgenson, Dale W., and B. M. Fraumeni. 1992. "Investment in Education and U.S. Economic Growth." *Scandinavian Journal of Economics,* 94: 51–70.

Koc, Fatos. 2014. *Sovereign Asset and Liability Management Framework for Debt Management Offices: What Do Country Experiences Suggest?*: UNCTAD.

Kunte, A., K. Hamilton, J. Dixon, and M. Clemens. 1998. "Estimating National Wealth: Methodology and Results. Environment Department Paper 57." *World Bank.*

Lange, Glenn-Marie, Quentin Wodon, and Kevin M. Carey, ed. 2018. *The changing wealth of nations 2018. Building a sustainable future.* Washington, DC, USA: World Bank Group.

Looman, Volker. 2006. "Die Vermögensfrage. Einkommen und Konsum sind die Eckpfeiler der Privatbilanz." *Frankfurter Allgemeine Zeitung GmbH*(15.01.2006). https://www.faz.net/ aktuell/finanzen/fonds-mehr/die-vermoegensfrage-einkomme n-und-konsum-sind-die-eckpfeiler-der-privatbilanz-1305937. html.

Lynch, Robin. 2018. "Intellectual Property in the national accounts. Paper prepared for the 35th IARIW General Conference." *IARIW.*

Mayer, Thomas. 2015. *Die neue Ordnung des Geldes. Warum wir eine Geldreform brauchen.* 2nd ed.

Mayer, Thomas. 2017. *Aktivgeld*: Flossbach von Storch Research Institute.

Mazzucato, Mariana. 2018. *The value of everything. Making and taking in the global economy.* London: Allen Lane an imprint of Penguin Books.

Measuring Worth. 2019. MeasuringWorth.com. https://www.measuringworth.com/calculators/uscompare/relativevalue.php (accessed July 24, 2019).

Meinen, Gerhard, Piet Verbiest, and Peter-Paul de Wolf. 1998. "Perpetual Inventory Method. Service lives, discard pattern and depreciation methods." *Statistics Netherlands, Department of National Accounts.*

Mercer. 2018. "Melbourne Mercer Global Pension Index 2018."

Minister of Finance, The people's Republic of China, and Japan Minister of Finance. 2018. "Joint Research Report on the Chinese and Japanese Pension system."

Ministry of Health and Social Affairs. 2016. "The Swedish old-age pension system. How the income pension, premium pension and guarantee pension work."

Ministry of SMEs and Startups. 2019. "Status of Korean SMEs." 2019.

Muller, Patrice, Anselm Mattes, Demetrius Klitou, Olivia-Kelly Lonkeu, Paula Ramada, Francisco Aranda Ruiz, Shaan Devnani, Johannes Farrenkopf, Agata Makowska, and Nadiya Mankovska, et al. 2018. *Annual report on EU small and medium-sized enterprises 2017/2018, Annual report on European SMEs 2017/2018. SMEs growing beyond borders.* [Luxembourg]: [Publications Office of the European Union].

National Association of Small and Medium Enterprise Promotion Organizations. 2018. *White Paper On Small And Medium Enterprises in Japan.*

National Pension Service. 2018. "National Pension Fund 2018 Annual Report."

Nikkei Asian Review. 2017. Japan Inc.'s pension obligations shrink for first time in eight years. https://asia.nikkei.com/Economy/Japan-Inc.-s-pension-obligations-shrink-for-first-time-in-eight-years (accessed September 28, 2019).

Nomura Research Institute. 2018. "Japan's Asset Management Business 2018/2019."

OECD. 2015. *OECD Studies on SMEs and Entrepreneurship: Russian Federation.* Washington: Organisation for Economic Co-operation and Development.

OECD. 2017a. *Entrepreneurship at a Glance 2017.* Paris: OECD Publishing.

OECD. 2017b. *The Size and Sectoral Distribution of State-Owned Enterprises*: OECD.

OECD. 2018a. "Pension Markets in Focus."

OECD. 2018b. *Pensions at a Glance Asia/Pacific 2018*: OECD.

OECD Statistics. 2019. OECD Statistics. https://stats.oecd.org/ (accessed July 4, 2019).

Pearce, David W. 1999. *Economics and environment. Essays on ecological economics and sustainable development.* Cheltenham: Elgar.

Penn World Tables. 2019. The Database | Penn World Table | Productivity | University of Groningen. https://www.rug.nl/ggdc/productivity/pwt/ (accessed July 4, 2019).

Pension Fund Regulatory & Development Authority. 2018. "Annual Report 2017-18."

Price Waterhouse Coopers. 2015. *State-Owned Enterprises. Catalysts for public value creation?*

Public Investment Corporation. 2018. "Driving the Achievement of SDGs by unlocking the ESG Risk Premium. Integrated Annual Report."

Robinson, Timothy P. 2011. *Global livestock production systems.* Rome: Food and Agriculture Organization of the United Nations.

Rosegrant, M. W., M. Agcaoili-Sombilla, and D. P. Nicostrato. 1995. "Global Food Projections to 2020: Implications for Investment."

Rosegrant, M. W., C. Ringler, S. Msangi, and et al. 2008. "International Model for Policy Analysis of Agricultural Commodities and Trade (IMPACT): Model Description." *IFPRI, Washington D.C.*

Scatigna, M., R. Szemere, and K. Tsatsaronis. 2014. "Weltweite Statistiken zu Wohnimmobilienpreisen."

Shorrocks, Anthony e. a. 2018. *Credit Suisse Global Wealth Report 2018*: Credit Suisse.

Siikamäki, J., F. J. Santiago-Avila, and P. Vail. 2015. "Global Assessment of Non-Wood Forest Ecosystem Services. Spatially explicit meta-analysis and benefit transfer to improve the World Bank's forest wealth database." *Program on Forests (PROFOR)*.

Singapore Department of Statistics. 2018. "Infographics - Singapore Economy."

SIPRI. 2018. "SIPRI Yearbook 2018 Summary."

SIPRI. 2019a. SIPRI databases | SIPRI. https://www.sipri.org/databases (accessed August 6, 2019).

SIPRI. 2019b. "SIPRI Yearbook 2019, Summary."

Smith, Robert H. T. 1970. "Concepts and Methods in Commodity Flow Analysis." *Economic Geography*, 46(Supplement: Proceedings. International Geographical Union. Commission on Quantitative Methods): 404–16.

Solow, Robert M. 1974. "Intergenerational Equity and Exhaustible Resources." *The Review of Economic Studies*, 41: 29.

Solow, Robert M. 1986. "On the Intergenerational Allocation of Natural Resources." *The Scandinavian Journal of Economics*, 88(1): 141–49.

StarCapital AG. 2019. Stock Market Valuation (P/B, 31.07.2019). https://www.starcapital.de/en/research/stock-market-valuation/ (accessed September 4, 2019).

Statistics Canada. 2019. Registered Pension Plans (RPPs), active members and market value of assets by contributory status. https://www150.statcan.gc.ca/t1/tbl1/en/cv.action?pid=1110010601 (accessed September 28, 2019).

Sundberg, Olle. 2018. *The Swedish pension system and pension projections until 20 7 0*: Government offices of Sweden.

Swedish Pensions Agency. 2018. "Orange Report 2018."

Swiss RE. 2018. "Pension schemes in Latin America: addressing the challenges of longevity."

The state council - The People's Republic of China. 2019. China's pension funds in stable condition: official. http://english.www.gov.cn/statecouncil/ministries/201909/25/content_WS5d8ac876c6d0bcf8c4c14024.html (accessed September 28, 2019).

The World Bank Group - www.worldbank.org. 2015. Global Consumption Database. http://datatopics.worldbank.org/consumption/ (accessed September 26, 2019).

Tiftik, Emre, and Khadija Mahmood. 2019. *High and Rising Debt Levels: Should we worry? Global Debt Monitor*: IIF - Institute of International Finance.

United Nations. 2019. System of Environmental Economic Accounting |. https://seea.un.org/ (accessed July 16, 2019).

United Nations et al. 2003. "Handbook of National Accounting. Integrated Environmental and Economic Accounting 2003."

United Nations et al. 2011. *System of national accounts 2008*. Washington, D.C., London: International Monetary Fund; Eurospan [distributor].

United Nations Statistics Division. 2019. UNSD — Welcome to UNSD. https://unstats.un.org/home/ (accessed July 4, 2019).

Viet, Vu Q. 2011. "Compiling GDP by final expenditure. An operational guide using commodity flow approach." *United Nations, National Bureau of Statistics of China.*

WhatCurrency.net. 2019. List Of Fiat Currencies 2019. https:// whatcurrency.net/world-fiat-money-list/ (accessed September 13, 2019).

Willis Towers Watson. 2018. "Global Pension Assets Study 2018."

World Bank. 2006. *Where is the Wealth of Nations? Measuring Capital for the 21ˢᵗ Century.* Washington, D.C.: World Bank.

World Bank. 2011. *Environment and development, The Changing Wealth of Nations. Measuring sustainable development in the new millennium.* Washington, D.C.: World Bank.

World Bank. 2019. Human Capital Project. https://www.world-bank.org/en/publication/human-capital (accessed September 18, 2019).

World Bank Data Catalog. 2019. Data Catalog | Data Catalog. https://datacatalog.worldbank.org/ (accessed July 4, 2019).

World Economic Forum. 2017. "We'll live to 100- How Can We Afford it?"

World Economic Forum. 2019. "Investing in our Future."

World Gold Council. 2019. Gold data. https://www.gold.org/ (accessed September 16, 2019).

Zakrzewski, Anna, and et al. 2018. *Global Wealth 2018. Seizing the Analytics Advantage*: The Boston Consulting Group (BCG).

13

Figures and tables